Telling a Neglected Story

Leadership of the African Methodist Episcopal Zion Church in Difficult Times

Rev. Dr. Cynthia Willis Stewart

Edited by Isabella Blanchard

Copyright Page

Copyright © 2013 by Cynthia W. Stewart

First Published in the United States by:

VTS Press
3737 Seminary Road
Alexandria, VA 22304
www.vts.edu

Edited by
Isabella Blanchard

Cover Design by
Thomas Zdancewiz

ISBN
978-0615841236
0615841236
Printed in the United States of America
Publication date August 2013
First Edition

Dedicated to the sainted memory of my mother and father.

ACKNOWLEDGEMENTS

I could not have completed this labor without the help of Ian Markham whose insightful and thoughtful comments have shaped this thesis. His tireless encouragement and ongoing support over many years despite a busy schedule brought this work to fruition. To Bishop Nathaniel Jarrett of the African Methodist Episcopal Zion Church, my heartfelt thanks for his superior editorial assistance. I thank Dr. Gregory Robeson Smith, Mr. David Caines and Mrs. Katherine Warren for their contributions of valuable information which helped me complete this work. Not least of all, thanks to my husband, Ronald, for his unwavering support.

I attribute to the African Methodist Episcopal Zion Church the source materials in Appendices
One, Two, Three, Four, Seven, Eight, Nine and Ten, Bishop Shaw's involvement in Establishing an Extension Seminary on and his expansionist activities.

I wish also to thank The National Association for the Advancement of Colored People, for authorizing the use of Appendices Five and Six and information regarding the letter to Bishop Walls from Channing Tobias.

TABLE OF CONTENTS

Introduction   1

Chapter One - The History of Methodism   8

Chapter Two - The African Methodist Episcopal ZionChurch   29

Chapter Three - Bishops, Leadership and the African Methodist Episcopal Zion Church   51

Chapter Four - Bishop William Jacob Walls: The Impact of His Life, Leadership and Legacy   60

Chapter Five - Bishop Stephen Gill Spottswood: The Impact of His Life, Leadership and Legacy   87

Chapter Six - Bishop Herbert Bell Shaw: The Impact of His Life, Leadership and Legacy   104

Conclusion   112

Appendix One - Letter from Bishop Walls to Young Pastor 118

Appendix Two - The Harriet Tubman Home 119

Appendix Three - Letter from Dr. Martin Luther King Jr. 125

Appendix Four - Victim of Envy, Slain by Talent by Bishop Walls 127

Appendix Five - Sample of Bishop Spottswood's Schedule 130

Appendix Six - Spottswood's Keynote address as President, NAACP National Board of Directors 134

Appendix Seven - Address by Spottswood: Building and Using the Power of the Ghetto 150

Appendix Eight - Sermon by Bishop Spottswood 156

Appendix Nine - Sermon by Bishop Herbert Bell Shaw 161

Appendix Ten - Episcopal Address by Bishop Shaw 165

Bibliography 183

TELLING A NEGLECTED STORY

INTRODUCTION

This work focuses on the African Methodist Episcopal Zion Church, a major historic Black Christian denomination which has long been ignored as a subject of serious academic reflection. An examination of twenty publications substantiates this view.[1] In these works, the approach taken is almost exclusively

---

[1] Publications examined were: 1] Ivan Lee Holt. The Methodists of the World. (New York: Editorial Department, Board of Missions and Church Extension of the Methodist Church) 1950 – A few references; 2] History of American Methodism - Relatively good source; 3] Edward L. Queen II et al, Editors, Martin E. Marty Editorial Adviser. Encyclopedia of American Religious History Third Edition. (132 West 31st Street, New York 1001: Facts on file, Library of American History. Inc.), 2009 – Poor, One Column; 4] Henry Warner Borden and P.C. Kenney, Editors. American Church History. (Nashville: Abingdon Press), 1998 – Early Black church mentioned, nothing of the AME Zion Church by name – Poor; 5] Mark A. Nell. A History of Christianity in the United States and Canada. (Grand Rapids, Michigan: William B. Eerdman's Publishing Company) 1992 - about four or five times within lines – Poor; 6] Leonard Woolsey Bacon: A History of American Christianity. (New York: The Christian Literature Company) 1897 – Not included – Poor; 7] William Warren Sweet. Religion of the American Frontier 1783-1840: Vol. IV. (New York, NY: Cooper Square Publishers, Inc.) 1964 – not mentioned Poor; 8] Lawrence Neale Jones. African Americans and the Christian Churches 1619-1860. (Cleveland: The Pilgrim Press) 2007 - 24 pages Good; 9] Timothy E. Fulop & Albert J. Raboteau (Editors). African –American Religion: Interpretive Essays in History & Culture. (New York: Routledge) 1977 – Interspersed; 10] Theophus H. Smith. Conjuring Culture: Biblical Formations of Black America. (New York: Oxford University Press) 1984 – Not mentioned – Poor; 11] Clifton Olmstead. History of Religions in the United States. (Englewood Cliffs, NJ: Prentice Hall, Inc.) 1960 - did not merit mention in index but was mention was elicited in one paragraph; 12] Jerald C. Brauer. Protestantism in America. A Narrative History. (Philadelphia: The Westminster Press) 1953 – Not mentioned even though the material dealt with schisms among Methodists; 13] Wardell J. Payne. Directory of African Religious Bodies: A Compendium of the Howard University School of Divinity. (Washington, DC: Howard University Press) 1995 – Good source; 14] Emory Steven Burke, General Editor et al. The History of American Methodism. Vol. III (New York: Abingdon Press) 1964. A total of about two pages; 15] Frederick A. Norwood. The Story of American Methodism: A History of the United Methodists and Their Relations. (New York: Abingdon Press), 1974 – About 11 pages, Good; 16] John G. McEllhenney et al (Editors). United Methodists In America: A Compact History. Nashville: Abington Press, 1982 – Poor, mentioned in passing. 17] Winthrop S. Hudson: Religion in America: An Historical Account of the Development of American Religious Life. (New York: MacMillan Publishing Company,) 1992 – Sight mention, Poor; 18] Milton C. Sernett (Editor). African American Religious History: A Documentary Witness. (Durham, NC: Duke University Press) 1999 – Fair source; 19] Edwin Gaustad & Leigh Schmidt. The Religious History of America: The Heart of the American Story from Colonial Times to Today. (San Francisco, CA: Harper Collins) 2002 – one reference, Poor; 20] Sydney E. Ahlstrom. A Religious History of the American People. (New Haven: Yale University Press) 1972. Very Limited reference, Poor.

1

sociological. Having served in ministry in excess of three decades and as a Pastor and a Presiding Elder for several years provided numerous opportunities for listening to seasoned pastors and leaders speak again and again of venerated members of the church as inspiring leaders, often of revered memory, as though they yet existed. Whether spoken, written, or studied, all agreed it is clear that in order to have effective ministry (lay or clergy), accomplished leadership is a must.

We must couch the history in such a way that it will motivate and inspire its readers to draw from within themselves and realize that they can, like so many of the fathers and mothers of the Church gone before them, become leaders in their communities. Regrettably, the history of the A.M.E. Zion Church has long been ignored as a subject of serious academic reflection, limiting the leadership resources available to young members of the Church. David H. Bradley, Secretary, Historical Society of the A.M.E Zion Church made a similar observation some 52 years ago when he wrote, "A careful survey of several leading libraries show little or no mention of the A.M.E. Zion Church."[2]

The approach taken here is almost pre-modern, in the sense that the purpose behind writing about the past is not simply to report what happened, but to inspire readers to think critically about the challenges and nature of leadership. The case can be made that such an approach is an intrinsic part of any writing about African American history. Neutrality is impossible and interpretation is inevitable, but regardless, in order to educate the A.M.E. Zion community, access to history must be the first step. It was William Wells

---

2   David H. Bradley <u>Report of the A.M.E. Zion Historical Society June 1958- May 31-1959.</u> Board of Bishops & The Connectional Council of The A.M.E. .ZION Church, Springfield, Mass. July 30, 1959.

Brown, a runaway slave and later abolitionist, who in 1874 wrote one of the first 'race' histories. Stephen Hall explains:

> Race histories, including Brown's, not only mapped their racial past, but instilled pride and provided a roadmap for how the race might adapt to freedom. Re-creating the past to inform the present proved important, but in order to facilitate adaption to freedom, it was necessary to look into the future. In charting the future by reconfiguring the past, Brown's work placed less emphasis on the harshness of the slave regime and focused instead on the varied ways African Americans resisted its most damaging effects. Rather than harsh masters and compliant slaves, Brown presented interracial dramas of aggressive agitation against the slave regime. He presented freedom as a teleological process and as a moment of unfettered possibility.[3]

Brown's approach to history is one that has continued to the present day in the African American tradition. It is my fervent hope to maintain, and further, that tradition. The story of the past must be written to inspire new leadership in the future.

The African Methodist Episcopal Zion Church has achieved global status now, but her sons and daughters must first and foremost realize that this denomination was not born in a vacuum and it is, therefore, necessary that the history of Methodism be visited and a brief look at the current Methodist family in America be examined before reflecting on the birth and history of the denomination. In an effort to motivate and inspire through history, three

---

[3] Stephen G. Hall, Faithful Account of the Race: African American Historical Writing in Nineteenth-Century America, (Chapel Hill: The University of North Carolina Press 2009), p.2. For Brown see William Wells Brown, The Rising Son; or, Antecedents of the Colored Race (1874).

of Zion's icons will be examined in terms of their leadership styles and legacy, and their indelible imprint on the Civil Rights movement in the United States of America. The intention of this examination is to engage the community of scholars and act as catalyst to further study of this denomination, and the history of a church that serves over a million members worldwide.

In the interest of accuracy, it must be acknowledged that there is a vast lack of denominational archives; historical inventory and archival storage is nearly non-existent, and that those who do have resources (outside of the major few), often hold on to them silently, lest they be taken away and not shared, or, in the worst case, be stolen or lost, as has been the case on occasion. Moreover, just when all and sundry were finally awakening and endeavoring to take steps to move towards (even if this meant to creep) meeting the needs of a much improved, much modernized, well financed and staffed archival system, we fell into an economic depression. Suffice it to say, the problem of accessible data remains massive.

Just how appalling the need for archival resources is was recognized as far back as 52 years ago when the denomination's historical society's budget was a meager $20,000/quadrennial. Said the then Historical Society's Secretary, Dr. David H. Bradley:

> We call attention to the fact that daily much extreme value to our people is slipping away into areas where it becomes merely hear-say. We have noted before that precious little is to be found in the great libraries of our nation on the African Methodist Episcopal Zion Church. *We cannot depend much longer on memory to fill the gaps of our records.* Then, too, the dangers of this type of source are all too apparent. We caution, too, against unsupported claims which may place the

denomination in an unenviable position in years to come. As far as we are able we should see to it that as much of our history as possible is well documented.[4] (Italics added)

This, if nothing else, gives cause to the plea to 'save the story'; certainly, it should be a greater priority in our tradition. Even today, much of our history exists only in oral tradition and remains inaccessible to those outside of the culture. Technology is advancing rapidly, putting our written work and few paper records in jeopardy, but paper at jeopardy would be preferred to none at all. Local historians are needed in each church before the opportunity to create a comprehensive story of the African Methodist Episcopal Zion Church is lost completely.

Archival work has been a very low priority in almost all Black churches. As a result, very few Black churches have adequate archival resources. Compounding this situation is the fact that of the Blacks who have been fortunate in access to higher education, relatively few have the financial luxury of researching and writing on the history of their denomination. The struggle of eking out a living that would allow one to take a reasonably good position in the community and be able to sustain a family again left church history at the low end of the priority list. The majority-White churches have made archival records a priority. It is the major reason why the histories on American religion focus on the story of the mainline: Catholic and Southern Baptists. The result is that the story of America's past is distorted. We need Black churches to keep the record. Lincoln and Mamiya were correct in their estimation that:

because there has been such a dearth of serious research on

---

4   Ibid

black churches up to very recent times, the Black Church has often experienced difficulty in conceptualizing or knowing itself except as an amorphous, lusterless detail on some larger canvas devoted to other interests. In consequence the Black Church has often found itself repeating history it had already experienced, and relearning lessons it had long since forgotten.[5]

It becomes clear that the consequences of racism reverberate through the centuries. For all the progress in the present, the past remains captive to a racism that shapes our collective story. For the large, predominantly White denominations, the record of the past has been collected, stored, and is constantly available. For historically Black denominations, the past was not collected or stored, and therefore is much harder to make available. The need exists not merely for a body of knowledge of what was, but indeed to help make the past so clear that as individuals, as a people, it will be ever woven in the fabric of our lives. In the work place or the church, we must be always conscious of the history shaping our tradition.

Naturally, a work of this nature cannot explore all the economic and social issues that shape the telling of this story. Many of the great African Methodist Episcopal Zion Churches are in neighborhoods that have been transformed. Affordable housing in many of the great urban centers of the United States has disappeared. As a result, some of these congregations struggle. Instead of participating in the affluence, the African American community is forced to move out. This economic and social reality needs to be part of this narrative, but it is beyond the focus of this particular work.

---

5   C. Eric Lincoln and Lawrence H. Mamiya. <u>The Black Church in the African American Experience.</u> (Durham, North Carolina: Duke University Press, 1990), p. 4

TELLING A NEGLECTED STORY

This particular work is looking at a connection to Methodism. And so, we start by reflecting on the history of Methodism, for the African Methodist Episcopal Zion Church stands firmly on the Methodist foundation. Indeed, one of its twenty-first century bishops makes this very clear:

> As I mentioned before in my address to you, I am still intentional and determined to have Methodist churches in my Episcopal District. Methodist implies and insists on a Method for doing what we do, and that method must be patterned, not on or of your own home spun methods, but by the Discipline of Methodism passed on to us by our Founder, John Wesley. After you have perfected all of the methods of "Pure Methodism", then I may tolerate some of your own, but not until you have convinced me that you have perfected ... that ... contained in our book of Discipline.[6]

---

[6] Bishop James E. McCoy: Episcopal Address 2009, (Alabama –Florida Episcopal District, African Methodist Episcopal Zion Church. 2009.

CHAPTER ONE
HISTORY OF METHODISM

Bishop Charles C. Selecman endorsed the notion that "the average Methodist needs and desires a concise account of the story of his Church,"[7] both local and denominational. Regardless of the tenets of Methodism to which one subscribes, "in order to understand The Methodist Church…it is important to know something of the Wesley family."[8] This chapter does not provide an all-encompassing discussion of the birth of Methodism, but only sets the stage for the subsequent history of the African Methodist Episcopal Zion denomination. It is instructive to point out that while now in existence on all continents of the world, Methodism started in England. John Wigger puts it succinctly:

> British Methodism…grew rapidly in the late eighteenth and early nineteenth centuries exerting a powerful influence on the societies and cultures in which it flourished. The spiritual journey of Methodism's founder, John Wesley (1703-1791) began early in life and took him through several stages.[9]

Wigger suggests that the denomination "grew rapidly in the late eighteenth and early nineteenth centuries" implying a prior existence of

---

7   George H. Jones (Editor), The Methodist Primer, (Nashville, Tennessee: Methodist Evangelistic Material, ND) 5, 1945
8   Ibid, p.7
9   John H. Wigger, Taking Heaven by Storm: Methodism and the Rise of Popular Christianity in America, (Urbana, Illinois: University of Illinois Press, 1998), 13.

Methodism and not one created or brought into reality by Wesley, though indeed, his contribution to the tradition justifies the assumption so widely held by many Methodists and non-Methodists alike that it was his methodical habits that gave birth to the denomination. Several authors support this. Said John A. Vickers:

> The term [Methodism] has a lengthy pedigree. JW (John Wesley) himself traced it back to a first century school of medicine, though the link is tenuous. More plausibly, he saw it as referring to the 'regular method of study and behavior' adopted under his leadership by the Holy Club. He himself had begun to be methodical during his student days monitored in the diary he began to keep.[10]

In his chapter on Methodism and the Christian Heritage in England, Richard Heitzenrater discussed the Puritans, Arminians, Roman Catholics, the Act of Uniformity and other parliamentary measures used by Queen Elizabeth I to settle the religious questions of the day, none of which were appreciated. The roaring arguments over all this led to the coining of the term Methodism:

> the Puritans at times seemed to be "proving" (if not earning) their salvation by their good works. The Arminians were not claiming any meritorious value for "good works" either; but were emphasizing the human opportunity to accept the empowerment of God's grace. The primacy of grace was central to their position, though the implication of divine/human cooperation (synergism), led many to criticize the Arminians for stressing human activity in salvation. The controversies that developed over this issue toward the end

---

10 John A Vickers (Editor), A Dictionary of Methodism in Britain and Ireland, (Great Britain: Biddles Ltd, Guildford and King's Lynn, 2000), 230.

of the seventeenth century led to some interesting "name-calling" that is of importance to an understanding of the name "Methodists." As early as the 1670s, both in the Low Countries and in England, a few orthodox Calvinists began to write vigorously against the Arminians and their "new method" of doing theology, especially relative to their views of justification and sanctification. Those designated as "New Methodists," persons using this new (i.e. wrong) method...[11]

In the introduction of his book, *The Journal of John Wesley*, Christopher Idle referred to the Oxford group nicknamed the Methodists, and said of the Wesleys: "[they] led the way here (the younger brother Charles being the first Methodist in conversion...)."[12] Also addressing the outgrowth of Methodism was E. Franklin Jackson who describes it as having been founded by:

> John and Charles Wesley, who, at Christ College, Oxford University, in England, began a "Holy Club," as it was called, for the express purpose of reading the Holy Scriptures, prayer and meditation. Because of the systematical manner in which they went about their religious practices, they were nicknamed Methodist, and as the movement grew the name were adopted. It might be said that these consecrated men hoped to revitalize the Anglican Church, but when their efforts were opposed and they were not permitted to carry out their ideals in the Anglican Church, then and only then did they turn to the people and begin to preach and organize societies."[13]

Charles Wesley may have been first in conversion; he may have written

---

11 Richard P. Heitzenrater, Wesley and the People Called Methodists, (Nashville: Abingdon Press, 1995), 18.
12 Christopher Idle, The Journal of John Wesley, (Michigan: Lion Publication Corp. 1986), 7.
13 E. Franklin Jackson, D.D, My Church: Hand Book for A.M.E. Zion Churchmen, (Washington, D.C.: James A. Brown/John Wesley Church, 1953), 8.

hundreds of hymns, and he may have been the catalyst, but it is John Wesley to whom Methodism owes its roots.

John was named after his paternal grandfather, and like father, grandfathers and his brother Charles, was an ordained minister (of the Church of England). Both of John's parents were the children of ministers. John's father, the Reverend Samuel Wesley, "was the son of John Wesley and the grandson of Bartholomew Wesley, both of whom were graduates of Oxford and clergymen in the Church of England".[14] Meanwhile his mother was the "daughter of Dr. Samuel Annesley, an English clergyman".[15]

John was born on June 17, 1703 in the parsonage in Epworth, England where his parents lived and his father served. He died in London in his eighty-eighth year on March 3, 1791. After spending his first ten years at the rectory in Epworth, England, John spent his adolescence at the Charterhouse school in London where his teachers "built on the foundations his mother had laid and prepared him for his years at Christ Church, Oxford."[16]

Historians note that while at the University of Oxford, John developed a rigorous daily plan of study which included: "Mondays and Tuesdays, Greek and Latin; Wednesdays, logic and ethics; Thursdays, Hebrew and Arabic; Fridays, Metaphysics and Natural Philosophy; Saturdays, Oratory and Poetry; [and] Sunday, Divinity."[17] John Wesley graduated from Oxford University and in that same year, on September 19, 1725 was ordained a Deacon. The following year he was "elected a fellow of Lincoln College, Oxford... and awarded the

---

14   George H. Jones (Editor), The Methodist Primer, (Nashville, Tennessee: Methodist Evangelistic Material, ND), 7.
15   Ibid.
16   Ibid., 379
17   George H. Jones (Editor), The Methodist Primer, (Nashville, Tennessee: Methodist Evangelistic Material, ND), 9.

degree of Master of Arts in 1727. He was ordained a Priest in the Church of England, September 22, 1728."[18]

Vickers and others explain that, following his ordination, John was often absent from college helping his father in his two Lincolnshire parishes. He returned to Oxford a year later to find his brother Charles, along with a few religious men, pursuing daily religious activities in a methodological manner which earned them the nicknames of 'Holy Club' and the 'Methodists'. Big brother John soon, more because of his inclinations and nature rather than his seniority, became the Holy Club's leader; preaching, teaching, and leading prayer. Regardless, Reverend John was yet to have that special relationship with God that Pentecostal and Evangelical Christians tend to have. Notwithstanding, Rev. John Wesley and his brother Rev. Charles, once they responded to God's call, worked arduously for God and His kingdom. Indeed, he is credited with saying:

> "Leisure and I have taken leave of each other." For more than fifty years he preached an average of three times a day, a total of 42,000 sermons. He often rode on horseback from sixty to seventy miles a day, covering in his land journeys 250,000 miles. When he was seventy-five years of age he speaks of having travelled 280 miles in forty-eight hours. He published 440 books, tracts, and pamphlets. [19]

Before dealing with Methodism and the shaping of this great church as it has evolved today, it is imperative that one looks at Wesley's progress in his own salvation. Initially,

> his...methods and activities perhaps best characterized as meditative piety, were all designed to promote "holiness of

---

18 Ibid.
19 Ibid.

heart and life"... At that time, Wesley's hope for salvation was grounded in reliance upon the sincerity of his own desire to lead the Christian life and a trust in God's promises as he understood them.[20]

Much remains to be said of the character of Methodism and the things that gave rise to its form then and now. Indeed, Walls in his description referred to Methodism as

> a spiritual movement in the temporal environment. These would be cold words if they were not built upon hearts pregnant with celestial fire and hand and bodies absorbed in a wholehearted trial to fulfill and expand the spirit and fervency of this potent reality of divine presence and meaning in the concrete environment.

Indeed, one of necessity must examine Wesley's heartwarming experience, since it leads to a better understanding of his description of a Methodist.

As the story goes, General James Oglethorpe was organizing a colony in Georgia and required a number of clergymen to minister to the spiritual needs of the colonists and serve as missionaries to the Native Americans. Whether he believed that religion was the opiate of the masses or had a genuine concern for the spiritual welfare of the colonists remains unclear. Regardless, John Wesley volunteered to serve in the mission field and his brother Charles as the General's Secretary.

---

[20] Richard P. Heitzenrater. <u>Wesley and the People Called Methodists.</u> (Nashville: Abingdon Press, 1995), 43.

Cynthia Lynn Lyerly points out that "to write about Methodist beginnings in America (a past Northern and Southern Methodists shared) is to enter a world of both fact and myth."[21] There is little doubt that myth is mixed with fact, but tradition says that on October 21, 1735, General Oglethorpe, John and Charles Wesley and about 80 other English and 26 Moravians, including women and children, set sail aboard the Simmonds bound for Georgia. It was in the course of the crossing that the Moravians made an ineffaceable impact upon John Wesley. They were said to be very pious and to have a simple but strong faith in God. As they traveled, storms arose and rocked the ship with a fierceness that drove rampant fear into the colonists' hearts. The Moravians, however, showed an absence of fear and through singing, prayer and the reading of scripture, displayed a paramount faith in God. John's eyes were opened to a new kind of Christian experience which he felt had been absent in his life.

It is reported that John was received well by most of the people in Georgia and that he worked assiduously at his ministry. Not only did he preach and administer the sacraments of the Church of England in English, but also in German, French, Italian and Spanish! Even here, his methodological inclinations surfaced, for he is said to have organized a society of the more studious and serious members of his parish and patterned it after the Holy Club. Indeed, it is said that after his return to England, he referred to this society that he established as the first Methodist Society after Oxford.

With regard to his work with the Indians, his great expectations proved less fruitful:

He thought he would find them [the Indians] with open minds,

---

21   Cynthia Lynn Lyerly, Methodism and the Southern Mind 1770-1810, (New York: Oxford University Press, 1998), 12

"as little children willing to learn and eager to do the will of God." To use his own words, however, they were "gluttons, thieves, liars, and murderers." They were so well content with their manner of living that they would brook no interference by Wesley nor permit him to come among them. The leaders told Wesley that they were too busily engaged with wars to hear him. All of Wesley's advisers, including Oglethorpe, insisted that the time had not yet come to establish a Christian mission among the Indians. He was greatly disappointed, for he considered the mission to the Indians his chief duty to America.[22]

This was not Wesley's only problem in his Georgia parish, nor was it his most telling. When it came to church discipline, Wesley's strict and unadulterated preaching of the Word offended the colonists. This coupled with his problems with the Indians and the fact that he did not agree to serve permanently as a priest for the Church of England in Georgia resulted in a discouraged John Wesley setting sail to return to England on December 22, 1737. Little did he realize the mark he had made in Georgia. George Whitefield is said to have later visited Georgia and commented on the excellent work that Wesley had done, the unyielding groundwork that he had laid and how precious his name was among the people: "the good John Wesley has done in America is inexpressible. His name is very precious among the people and he has laid a foundation that I hope neither man nor devils will ever be able to shake." [23]

A persistently disturbed-in-mind and restless-in-spirit John arrived in London February 3, 1738. He went about doing that which was set before him,

---

22   George H. Jones (Editor), <u>The Methodist Primer,</u> (Nashville, Tennessee: Methodist Evangelistic Material, ND), 12.
23   <u>Ibid,</u> 13.

but seemingly, all he could reflect on was the peace and assurance of his Moravian friends on the boat, something greatly missing in his life. One Moravian, Peter Bohler, a leader in London talked often with John -- conversations which led him to a new understanding of saving faith.

Tradition holds that on the evening of May 24, 1738 John Wesley went to a Moravian society meeting, where Luther's preface to the Epistle to the Romans was being read, emphasizing the changes in heart and soul attainable through faith in Jesus Christ. It was on this occasion that John Wesley felt his heart strangely warmed: "I felt I did trust in Christ, Christ alone for salvation; and an assurance was given me, that he had taken away my sins, even mine, and saved me from the law of sin and death."[24] This earth-shattering event must have been what led John Wesley to state that "a Methodist is one who lives according to the method laid down in the Bible, "[25] emphasizing a conversion based upon a heartwarming experience.

And so, under such inauspicious circumstances, Methodism started, grew and spread all over England, and as its followers moved abroad, so did it catch afire.

Rev. Dr. Phillip Hardt[26] reviewed literature and came up with the factors he saw as contributing to the swell of Methodism. Key among these was the liberal spiritual atmosphere which allowed wide interpretation and freedom in behavior in the spiritual conditions of the Church of England, conditions similar to what existed in the United States. The growth and spread of Methodism is further due to Wesley's wisdom and pragmatism as he fostered

24 Ibid, 14.
25 W.J. Townsend, A New History Of Methodism, (London: Hodder and Stoughton, 1909), 140.
26 Rev. Dr. Philip F. Hardt, The Soul of Methodism: The class Meeting in Early New York City Methodism, (New York: University Press of America, Inc., 2000), 2-3.

itinerant field preaching and created the system lay preaching which proved vital to the expansion and propagation of the development of the denomination through the Methodist revival.

Rev. Dr. Hardt highlighted the fact that Wesley's organizational skills played a great role in the establishment and solidification of the movement:

> Notwithstanding these different understandings of the impetus for the founding of Methodism, scholars are agreed that the movement provided strong spiritual support to its members through its three primary pastoral structures. First of all, the society meeting brought together on a weekly basis all the Methodists in a particular town or city. Second, every society member was encouraged to join a small band for more intimate sharing. Third and last, every prospective and full member was required to attend a weekly class meeting in which members described their spiritual progress under the guidance of the class leader.[27]

The society meeting is said to have begun in 1739 in London when persons sought further instructions and explanations, having heard Wesley preach. These weekly meetings became a part of the structure of Methodism, especially as they grew and spread and an organizational format was needed. Rev. Dr. Hardt's[28] description of the Society in Britain pointed out that Wesley "drew upon the earlier Anglican "religious society" in several ways."[29] As a result of John's contemplation and deliberation, the Wesleys (and no doubt those with whom they consulted) developed and wrote what is now known as the Discipline, for use by all Methodist societies.

The rules that Wesley instituted governed admission, attendance,

---

27 Ibid., p.7
28 Ibid, 7-47.
29 Ibid, 8.

frequency of meetings, conditions for expulsion and members' behavior. It is worth noting that these were all but 14 of the 39 general rules which govern the Anglican Church in England, where Wesley held his membership. Moreover, the 25 articles of religion of the Methodist Church are the same 25 that govern the African Methodist Episcopal Zion Church, not the least of which is the one condition still required of those who seek membership in a Methodist Society – "a desire to flee from the wrath to come and be saved from their sins."[30]

African Methodist Episcopal Zion scholar Atheal Pierce [31] holds the position that the Methodist faith is distinguishable from other protestant faiths. As he states: "The most fundamental distinction of Methodist teaching is that people must use logic and reason in all matters of faith. Also important is the acknowledgement of "prevenient," "justifying," and "sanctifying" grace. Methodism taught that all are blessed with these graces at different times through the power of the Holy Spirit." Pierce also addresses the pivotal role of the presence and actions of the Holy Spirit:

> Wesley sought a scriptural Christianity "energized" by the ongoing presence of the Holy Spirit. Wesley's theology addressed the issue of sin wherever it was found. He sought restoration of relationships between man and man and God and man. Wesley's theology addressed both the spiritual and social conditions of humanity. This was evidenced by the large response of the poor to his message and ministry. Early Methodism also had a strong evangelical fervor. Wesley taught that the major cause of social ills resulted from man's broken relationship with his Creator.[32]

---

30 George H. Jones (Editor), The Methodist Primer (Nashville, Tennessee: Methodist Evangelistic Material, ND), 17
31 Atheal Pierce, Ph.D. Methodists: Living our Beliefs. (A Presentation to the 114th Annual Central Alabama Conference School of Prophets), Clinton Chapel African Methodist Episcopal Zion Church 4640 Narrow Lane Road, Montgomery, Alabama 36116, October 15, 2009, 2.
32 Ibid. 3.

Each society, for members only, met in the evening and included exhortation, prayer, scriptural reading and a psalm. Unlike today, it is reported that each society was required to split into two when it reached a membership of 40. Until the very recent past, class tickets were given out once a quarter to those in good standing and one could not partake in Holy Communion unless one had attended the class meeting and could present the ticket. The discipline addressed the issue of non-attendance and moral behavior which were included in the rules as reasons for expulsion from societies and churches. Like today, probationary periods of training were compulsory for new members before full membership could be attained. The society's meeting included a talk as well as prayer, spiritual reading, a psalm and the asking of that vital question: "Is it well with your soul?"

It should be noted that the initial structure, which also included the band meeting, was apparently borrowed with some modification from the Moravians. Each band had a leader and at some point in the month leaders met to discuss their members. The band meeting also provided tickets for those who attended Moravian Love Feasts and thus were approved to participate in Holy Communion. It is reported that attendance and participation here was always low, though a necessity if one was to participate in the sacrament of Holy Communion.

The third structure established then and still functioning successfully in many branches of Methodism today is the class system. Many other denominations have borrowed this idea, called it by other names and used it successfully. It must be noted that the Wesleys never sought to establish Methodist churches, but merely wanted societies to attend their parish churches.

Tradition states that the class leader system was started for reasons other than a part of the organizational structure of a blossoming and spreading group called Methodists. Apparently when John Wesley's unit of Methodism became too large to manage, he broke it into small working units known as 'classes'. About the same time, the group owed on one of their meeting houses and sought ways to liquidate the debt. It was suggested that every member of the society give a penny a week, but many were too poor to pay even this meager amount. Thus, it was that a Captain Foy recommended that eleven of the poorest be put with him and he would then collect what they could give weekly, and make up for what and when they could not give. This was done. But as Basil Miller points out,

> When the stewards were visiting their eleven's for money purposes, they caught rumors of how the men were living. These lax conditions were reported to John, who like a flash saw the spiritual implications of this (small) group plan. Immediately, he called together the leaders of these financial classes, unfolded his scheme and told them to inform him as to how the people in their groups were living. In London the same plan was put into operation...when he called his leaders together and perfected his mobile working force...John soon found it practical for class leaders to visit each member at his own meeting at some central place which caused them "to bear one another's burdens"...And as they had daily a more intimate acquaintance, so they had a more endeared affection for each other.[33]

David Hempton summarized this for us ably:

> Bands and classes, hymns and love feasts, and rules and

---

33   Basil Miller, <u>John Wesley,</u> (Minneapolis, Minnesota: Bethany House Publishers, 1943), 82.

discipline supplied the requisite structure and rituals for reconstituted lives. In short Methodism evolved with a theology and structure that enabled it to meet the essential demands of individual assurance and communal discipline in a world order on the brink of very substantial changes. Methodism survived as the fittest of the various brands of evangelical piety in the first half of the eighteenth century, but its future growth depended largely on how well it would adapt to dramatic environmental changes.[34]

John Wesley is credited with directly influencing the growth of Methodism both in England and America, though he was seemingly unaware of the vastness of his influence on the latter. He is credited with laying the foundation in both countries, though he had left America with a broken heart and a feeling of total failure at the work he had done. Andrews credits the first Americans called "Methodists" as followers of George Whitefield, who earlier in this paper was quoted as crediting Wesley with laying a good foundation. Said Andrews:

> In time Methodism would flourish in the America's setting as it did in Britain, but this was unforeseen by its founder. John Wesley considered his Georgia mission a failure. Stymied by his parishioners' recalcitrance, his own rigid attachment to Anglican ceremony, and his inability to attract more than the Chickasaws' token interest in Anglicanism, Wesley had given up trying to convert the colonies. Instead, the first Americans called "Methodists" were followers of George Whitefield, the Wesleys' evangelical comrade and Calvinist competitor, who dominated American Methodism until the arrival of Wesley's itinerants in the Middle Colonies in 1769. [35]

---
34   David Hempton, Methodism: Empire of the Spirit, (New Haven, Connecticut: Yale University Press, 2005), 16.
35   Dee E Andrews, The Methodists and Revolutionary America, 1760-1800: The Shaping

Several versions of myths and facts blend to help us perceive the picture. "Between 1770 and 1820 American Methodists achieved a virtual miracle of growth, rising from fewer than 1,000 members to more than 250,000, by 1812 Methodists numbered one out of every 36 Americans. By 1830 membership stood at nearly half a million."[36]

Phillip Embury and Robert Strawbridge, two Methodist preachers in Ireland came to America in 1760. Embury is said to have "organized the first Methodist Society in New York in 1766 (while) Strawbridge organized the first Methodist Society in Maryland probably sometime during the year 1763."[37]

Shortly before the American Revolution, Methodism spread to the North American colonies. Lay immigrants brought the Methodist movement's teachings and disciplines. Their enthusiasm for their faith led them to gather small groups who met regularly to pray, sing and witness. "Methodist societies" were formed throughout the colonies, especially in Delaware, Maryland, New Jersey, New York, North Carolina, Pennsylvania and Virginia. Methodist preaching and teaching had a broad appeal for Wesley's followers proclaimed the gospel is for everyone. In response to the colonists' request, Wesley appointed two missionaries in 1769 to organize Methodism in America. Members were still requested to receive sacraments from Church of England clergy. Following the Revolutionary War, few Church of England priests remained in America. Wesley ordained two lay preachers and "set apart," Thomas Coke and Francis Asbury, as joint superintendents. Asbury sent Freeborn Garrettson and Harry "Black Harry" Hosier to gather the preachers, and on Christmas Eve 1784, the

---

of an Evangelical Culture, (Princeton, New Jersey: Princeton University Press, 2000), 3.
36   John H. Wigger, Taking heaven By Storm: Methodism and the Rise of Popular Christianity in America, (Urbana, Illinois: University of Illinois Press, 2001), 3.
37   George H. Jones (Editor), The Methodist Primer, (Nashville, Tennessee: Methodist Evangelistic Material, ND), 9.

TELLING A NEGLECTED STORY

Methodist Episcopal Church was organized in Baltimore.[38]

Jones et al[39] pointed out that in the 1760s British troops were in New York, and among them was one Captain Thomas Webb. Captain Webb had been converted in England under the preaching of John Wesley and had joined a Methodist Society and was a lay preacher. He proved to be Embury's 'right hand' in the building of the first New York Methodist Meeting House which was dedicated on October 30, 1768. It was Webb and others who made several appeals to Wesley for preachers. In response, Richard Wright and Francis Asbury were sent. Only one of the lot, Strawbridge, was ordained, and probably by a German minister. Not only were the colonists separated from England after the Revolutionary War, but most of the Anglican Priests returned to England. Who would administer the Methodists their sacraments? Many a distress call went to Wesley.

> Therefore, after calm deliberation, on September 1, 1784, assisted by Thomas Coke and James Creighton, also Presbyter of the Church of England, he (John Wesley) ordained Richard Whatcoat and Thomas Vasey deacons. The next day he ordained them elders. Then, assisted by Creighton, Whatcoat, and Vasey, he ordained Thomas Coke, Superintendent.[40]

The ordained immediately came to America and a Christmas conference of all preachers was called on December 24, 1784, resulting in Asbury and Coke being elected superintendents; the church being formally organized and named

---

38   Ruth A. Daugherty, General Commission on Christian Unity and Interreligious Concerns, UMC in Pan Methodist Commission, One Voice for Christ: The Wesleyan Family, (Charlotte, North Carolina, 2007), 2-3.
39   George H. Jones (Editor), The Methodist Primer, (Nashville, Tennessee: Methodist Evangelistic Material), 19-21.
40   Ibid, 20.

Methodist Episcopal; Asbury being ordained Deacon on Saturday, Elder on Sunday, and consecrated superintendent (Bishop) on Monday; the Articles of Religion and the Sunday service prepared by John Wesley for Methodists in North America being adopted; approval given for the establishment of a school, afterward known as Cokesbury College; twelve other preachers being elected and ordained Elders; and a program of Expansion outlined.

Hatch and Wigger emphasize the explosive growth of the Methodist Episcopal Church which was almost extinct in 1771 (four ministers and 3000 lay people) to about 34 per cent of all church people in 1850.

> Under the tireless direction of Asbury, the Methodists advanced from Canada to Georgia emphasizing three themes that Americans found captivating: God's free grace, the liberty of people to accept or reject that grace, and the power and validity of popular religious expression –even among servants, women, and African Americans.[41]

This family grew exponentially. Then, even as the twig falls from the tree, is buried, sprout roots and develops into new plants, so did the Church. It grew such that today, the Methodist Family has grown well beyond the Methodist Episcopal Church. Indeed, the US Pan Methodist Commission provides a timeline for the twenty first century Methodist family.

TIMELINE[42"]

1738   John Wesley – renewal movement, Church of England
1760s Philip Embury, Barbara Heck and Robert Strawbridge
        –"Methodist Societies" in America

---

41   Nathan O. Hatch and John H. Wigger (Editors), <u>Methodism and the Shaping of America</u>, (Nashville, Tennessee: Kingswood Books, 2001),
47 Pan Methodist Commission, <u>One Voice for Christ: The Wesleyan Family,</u> Charlotte, North Carolina, woon), 7

1784	Christmas Conference – Freeborn Garrettson and Harry Hosier – Methodist Episcopal Church, Francis Asbury and Thomas Coke appointed joint superintendents.
1787	Richard Allen – African Methodist Episcopal Church, Philadelphia.
1796	James Varick – African Methodist Episcopal Zion Church, New York
1800	Martin Boeham and Philip Otterbein – Church of the United Brethren in Christ
1803	Jacob Albright – Evangelical Association (Evangelical Church).
1813	Union American Methodist Episcopal Church
1830	Methodist Protestant Church
1843	Wesleyan Methodist Church of America
1844	Methodist Episcopal Church, South
1860	Free Methodist Church of North America
1870	Colored Methodist Episcopal Church (Christian Methodist Episcopal Church)
1881	New Congregational Methodist Church
1894	Evangelical Methodist Church
1939	Methodist Episcopal Church, Methodist Protestant Church and Methodist Episcopal Church, South form Methodist Church
1946	Church of the United Brethren in Christ and Evangelical Church form Evangelic United Brethren Church

1968   Evangelical United Brethren Church and Methodist Church form the United Methodist Church

The African Methodist Episcopal Church

Dennis C. Dickerson,[43] the historiographer of the African Methodist Episcopal Church provides the pen portrait of the history of his denomination thusly:

> The African Methodist Episcopal (A.M.E.) Church emerged from the Free African Society, a mutual-aid organization former slave Richard Allen founded in 1787. A racial incident at Philadelphia's St. George Methodist Church convinced the itinerant Methodist preacher to start a branch of Methodism that practiced racial equality.
>
> In 1794, Allen led in building Philadelphia's Bethel African Methodist Episcopal Church. In 1816, he convened African-American Methodists from other mid-Atlantic communities to form the African Methodist Episcopal denomination and was consecrated its first bishop.
>
> The A.M.E. Church rapidly spread throughout the United States, Canada and Haiti. During the Civil War, A.M.E. missionaries traveled into the confederacy too draw new members. As membership swelled to 400,000 by 1880, A.M.E. in the United States, Canada and Haiti. During the Civil War, A.M.E. missionaries traveled into the Confederacy to draw new members. As membership swelled to 400,000 by 1880, A.M.E. clergy and lay leaders became active politically.
>
> Reunification in 1884 with the British Methodist Episcopal Church added the Maritime Provinces, Bermuda and parts of South America. Formal entry into West Africa and South Africa in the 1890's expanded the denomination beyond the Western Hemisphere. Missionaries also embraced much of the Caribbean, especially Cuba.

---

[43]   Ibid.,2.

By 1900 several states, as well as the Caribbean and Africa, contained A.M.E.-supported schools on secondary, college, university and seminary levels.

The two World Wars, which launched a Massive African-American movement from the South the northern and western cities spearheaded more development. Urban churches developed a social gospel that redefined A.M.E. ministry. Today with more than two million members in 7,000 congregations on four continents, the A.M.E. Church plays a role in sustaining the Allen tradition.

The Christian Methodist Episcopal Church

The Executive Secretary of the Christian Methodist Episcopal Church, Attorney Juanita Bryant[44] provides the pen portrait of the history of her denomination.

> The Colored Methodist Episcopal (C.M.E.) Church came into existence as a result of the movement from slavery to freedom. The Methodist Episcopal (M.E.) Church South was an outgrowth of Wesley's Methodism. Some Blacks, converted to Christianity by slave masters, accepted the Methodist doctrine as it was. However, the emancipation of Blacks from slavery created the desire by Blacks to have and control their own church.
>
> In 1870, 41 African-American men gathered in Jackson, Tennessee. With the advice and assistance of the white brethren of the M.E. Church South, the Black religious leaders organized the colored branch of Methodism. They adopted the Methodist Church, South's Book of Discipline, and elected two of their own preachers – William H. Miles of Kentucky and Richard H. Vander horst of Georgia – as their bishops.

---

44   Ibid.,4.

Bishop W. J. Walls made it clear, however, that in the twentieth century Methodism today, on both sides of the ocean, has become afflicted with an icy dullness, and to put it more tritely, a splendid nullity. British Methodism has already voted to go back to the Anglican Church and American Methodism is struggling hard to overcome herself, the power that would crucify her on a cross of gold.[45]

45　　Bishop W.J. Walls The A.M.E. Zion Church: IT'S METHODIST IDENTITY (Salisbury, North Carolina: Livingstone College), July 31, 1966.

CHAPTER TWO

THE AFRICAN METHODIST EPISCOPAL ZION CHURCH

Initially, I thought the key to writing about the history of this denomination would be painting a picture of the environment in which Zion emerged, and I shall. But Bishop James Walker Hood, in dealing with "God's purpose in Negro Church As Seen in the History of the Movement 1831-1918"[46], described America at that time as a place like no other in the world. He described Black delegates to the Ecumenical Conference of Methodism in London in 1881 as likely to be honored and given extraordinary attention. In America on the other hand, the entire race was excluded from the social and religious circle of other races - regardless of the individual's moral, material or intellectual worth. That said, in some cases, the Church was the only cross-racial venue that was not totally closed against the Blacks or between Blacks and Whites, but the treatment of the Blacks was terrible, the conditions intolerable, the differences were seemingly insurmountable. Thus as Hood puts it:

---

46 James Walker Hood,1831-1918 Sketch of the Early History of the African Methodist Episcopal Zion Church with Jubilee Souvenir And Appendix: Electronic Edition © This work is the property of the University of North Carolina at Chapel Hill. It may be used freely by individuals (title page)

> Near the close of the eighteenth century, there began an unparalleled movement, which has resulted in the establishment of the Negro Church, not one branch merely, but all the branches; not of one denomination, merely, but of all denominations. The colored members of the different Christian denominations, of one accord, in all parts of the country, and as nearly as can now be learned, at about the same time, separated from the whites, and formed each for themselves, a church of the same faith and order, as those from which they separated, leaving the white churches almost without a colored membership. This is the movement which we have pronounced unparalleled.[47]

In spite of country-wide similarities in churches, conditions in the Northeastern city and state of New York where this denomination started must be observed more closely. Dr. James David Armstrong, Secretary, Historical Society of the African Methodist Episcopal Zion Church did a most effective job of this when in preparing a brief historical survey of the Church:

> Two years after 30 Dutch families settled on the island of Manhattan in 1624, 11 (eleven) Negro pioneers were imported to this new territory, which the Dutch had purchased from the Indians for "beads and trinkets," and named it "New Amsterdam". Servitude began immediately after their arrival when they were put to work as "company Negroes," building roads, cutting timber, clearing land, and erecting dwellings and forts. Eighteen (18) years after their arrival, the 11 Negro pioneers, with their families, boldly demanded freedom. Official tempers flared, but the rank-and-file of colonists recalled the early labors of these black men

---

[47] Ibid. p.60

and supported their demands. The authorities granted them land on the edge of the settlement; in a tangled swamp know today as Greenwich Village...By the first half of the eighteenth century, New York had the largest slave population north of the plantation states... In approaching the second half of the eighteenth century, the season of religious breakthrough for Africans in New York, one can easily observe the obstruction, the hindrance, and the barriers, which they would begin to challenge with insurmountable faith and courage, and finally make their move before the end of the century...Thus was the condition when the strange new sect from England, known by the name of Methodist, emerged on the American continent in the city of New York, 10 years later, and near the same period on the shores of Maryland, the suspicion and fear continued to exist with very little change until the Revolutionary War period. The handicaps under these pressures and oppressive laws were severe. In spite of this, a few free Africans managed to get enough education to read and write. Many of them were naturally skillful, full of God-given talents, and industrious in trade and occupations. This was typical of all the Africans, both slave and free, in all parts of the New Territory. Even though the strictest methods were used to keep them in ignorance and illiteracy, several incidents indicative of the skillful, tactful and intelligent Africans in this country are depicted by ... historical writers. Most miraculous of all this is how the African overcame a suffering handicap, long and inhumane, in comparison with the Indian whom the white man was never able to subject to slavery.[48]

---

48   James David Armstrong, <u>A Brief Historical Survey of the African Methodist Episcopal Zion Church</u> , (North Carolina: The A.M.E. Zion Historical Society, 2004) pp.2-3

When Methodism started in New York, though, Blacks were very much a part of the group:

> Philip Embury, who had been licensed by John Wesley, held the first Methodist meeting on American soil in his home in Augustus Street (then Barrack Street), exhorting to an audience of five, one black person was present. She was Betty, the slave of Barbara Heck, who had requested the meeting of her fellow countryman out of necessity to save their people from "hell." They sang and prayed while Mr. Embury instructed them in doctrines from salvation.[49]

The fact that "Negroes in New York were still not to have any known meeting among themselves unless otherwise supervised was a very perplexing situation, especially to the free group with a degree of education."[50] Yet it must be pointed out that this would not have been the case for Whites since the New York Post Boy of February 16, 1756 clearly states:

> Nine Negroes were recently "whipt at the whipping post" for illegally assembling on Sunday, February 8. Their offense was a violation of the provincial act aimed to prevent "the Conspiracy and Insurrection of Negroes and other slaves," and also of the city ordinance which required that not more than three Negroes should be seen together at one time, except in their owner's service, under penalty of being whipped.[51]

Free or slave, Blacks were all treated alike – negatively. It seems little wonder Blacks were drawn to Methodism initially, for John Wesley opposed

---

49   William J. Walls, <u>The African Methodist Episcopal Zion Church: The Reality of the Black Church,</u> (North Carolina: A.M.E. Zion Publishing House, 1974), p43
50   <u>Ibid.</u> p.39.
51   James David Armstrong, <u>A Brief Historical Survey of the African Methodist Episcopal Zion Church</u> , (North Carolina: The A.M.E. Zion Historical Society, 2004) p.3.

slavery and was "a friend of the black race long before it [Methodism] was introduced on the American continent."⁵² To put it in his words:

> By slavery I mean domestic slavery or that of a servant to a master. A late ingenious writer well observes, "The variety of forms in which slavery appears, makes it almost impossible to convey a just notion of it, by way of definition. There are however certain properties which have accompanied slavery in most places, whereby it is easily distinguished from that mild domestic service which obtains in our own country." All slave-holders of whatever rank and degree; seeing men-buyers are exactly on a level with men-stealers. Indeed you say, "I pay honestly for my goods: and I am not concerned to know how they are come by." Nay, but you are: You are deeply concerned; to know they are honestly come by. Otherwise you are partaker with a thief, and are not a jot honester than him. But you know they are not honestly come by: You know they are procured by means, nothing near as innocent as picking of pockets, house-breaking, or robbery upon the highway. You know they are procured by a deliberate series of more complicated villainy, of fraud, robbery and murder than was ever practiced either by Mahometans or Pagans: in particular by murders, of all kinds; by the blood of the innocent poured upon the ground like water. Now it is your money that pays the merchant, and thro' him the captain, and the African butchers. You therefore are guilty, yea, principally guilty, of all these frauds, robberies and murders. You are the spring that puts all the rest in motion: they would not stir a step without you:--Therefore the blood of all these wretches, who die before their time, whether in their country, or elsewhere lie upon your head. The blood of thy brother, (for, whether thou wilt believe it or not, such he is in the sight of him that made him) crieth against thee from

---

52 William J. Walls, The African Methodist Episcopal Zion Church: The Reality of the Black Church, (North Carolina: A.M.E. Zion Publishing House, 1974), p.32.

the earth, from the ship, and from the waters. O, whatever it costs, put a stop to its cry before it be too late. Instantly, at any price, were it the half of your goods, deliver thyself from blood-guiltiness! Thy hands, thy bed, thy furniture, thy house, thy lands are at present stained with blood. Surely it is enough; accumulate no more guilt; spill no more blood of the innocent! Do not hire another to shed blood: Do not pay him for doing it! Whether you are a Christian or no, shew yourself a man; be not more savage than a lion or a bear! Perhaps you will say, "I do not buy any Negroes: I only use those left me by my father."--So far is well; but is it enough to satisfy your own conscience? Had your father, have you, has any man living, a right to use another as a slave? It cannot be, even setting revelation aside. It cannot be that either war, or contract, can give any man such a property in another as he has in sheep and oxen. Much less is it possible, that any child of man should ever be born a slave. Liberty is the right of every human creature, as soon as he breathes the vital air. And no human law can deprive him of that right, which he derives from the law of nature. [53]

The history of Methodism reveals, however, that in spite of Wesley's views, few American Methodists were in concert with him, even though Blacks were a part of the American movement from its inception. One must not forget that the official public position of the Methodist church was anti-slavery. On the other hand, it cannot be forgotten that slavery played a role in the split of Methodism[54].

This should not be surprising, for as Walls points out, "all the Black churches were born in White congregations, East and West, North and South."[55]

53 John Wesley, Thoughts upon Slavery, (London, England: reprinted in Philadelphia, with notes and sold by Joseph Crukshank, MD, CC 1924) pp. 3; 54-56.
54 http://thebolesfamily.hubpags.com/hb/Slavery-and-the-Split-of-Methodism
55 William J. Walls, The African Methodist Episcopal Zion Church: The Reality of the Black

When the Blacks came as slaves, they had to divest themselves of everything but their lives and color. Meanwhile, many of the others who were brought to America as indentured immigrants or else kept their language and their contacts with others of their country, race or tribe. Oral history posits that slave traders had Blacks placed in the hold of ships in a manner which separated them such that no two who spoke the same dialect were housed together. This seemed to have been the pattern continued in homes, on plantations or wherever and in whichever countries Blacks were taken, forcing them to adopt the language of their owners. Walls in his wisdom wrote that "organized Christianity is the major thing the Black race got out of slavery, second to which was the English language. Slavery was a big price to pay, however, especially when we remember the boon of free civilization was granted to other branches of the human race without the blighting prolongation of slavery."[56]

The Methodist movement in America outgrew its humble beginnings in the Emburys' home and soon obtained a more commodious facility for meeting and a little later moved into the Rigging Loft at 120 William Street. The Black membership of John Street Church, in the beginning, was principally slave.

Blacks--slave and free--were initially permitted to occupy the back seats in the sanctuary. It may be of interest to note that these seats were spaced apart from each other, preventing contact between Black attendees. As membership grew, the Blacks were shuttled up to the gallery, and then to the back of gallery when, as the membership multiplied, White men had to take seats in the balcony, the capacity of the sanctuary being rather small. The Blacks were given

---

Church, (North Carolina: A.M.E. Zion Publishing House, 1974), p.21
56   Ibid.

communion after all Whites were served. They were baptized and named at the dictates of the White ministers who went so far as to re-name Black babies if they found the names given by parents not to their liking. As time went by, in spite of the harsh treatment and blatant indignities, some Blacks were licensed as local preachers. However, they were only permitted to preach occasionally, to Negroes only and when doing so, more often than not, they were given text and subject: "the colored preachers, were thus deprived of the opportunity of improving their gifts and graces, as they then stood connected with the white M.E. Society, and (most galling to those now viewing these events, they were) prohibited from joining the Annual M.E. Conference, as itinerant preachers, with their White brethren."[57] They were hard working men and women who attended church regularly and supported it financially and with labor, but could not be buried in a cemetery with white members! From the beginning of the Methodist Church in New York in 1766, at least one Black was present and an active part of the church. As the church grew so did the number of Blacks and their participation was not without fervor and enthusiasm, yet it would be thirty years before the people of color would choose--or circumstances force them to form their own church.

Generally, Zion's tradition seems to propagate the popular story of our forefathers marching forward and boldly starting the new denomination, and only when one gets to stages of greater interest or higher studies do further details become clear. Though tempted to follow tradition at this point and merely provide the flowery history of the African Methodist Episcopal Zion

---

57   Bishop John Jamison Moore, <u>History of the A.M.E Zion Church in America</u> (Charlotte, North Carolina: The A.M.E. Zion Historical Society, 2004), p. 4

TELLING A NEGLECTED STORY

Church as posited by some, scholarly integrity calls on us to acknowledge the fact that there are other voices which do not subscribe to this position, and in doing so demand another look at the historical facts.

Even after two centuries, the question is often debated as to what exactly was the catalyst that caused the Blacks to seek to form their own denomination. Hood gives us as clear a summary as one could ask when, as he explains, the extraordinary causes which gave rise to the movement could be applicable to all churches and are certainly applicable to African Methodist Episcopal Zion Church:

> Like causes produce like effects, wherever operated. Back seats, sometimes called "Nigger" pews, were provided for them. Galleries which were reached by outsteps, and in some cases, outside sheds were provided without any means of keeping warm, where they could hear the preacher, but could not see him. They were denied the privilege of the Lord's table, until all the whites had communed. The line of proscription was also drawn at the baptismal font. Such were some of the many vexations and indignities to which the colored members were subjected in the white church. Is it any wonder that they came out? The foregoing is what we find on the surface. But digging down, we shall find that what, on the surface of this subject appeared as only the result of a wicked proscription, born of race hate, begotten of that hydra-headed monster, American slavery, is only another of the many instances in which God his made the wrath of men to praise Him. [58]

---

58   James Walker Hood,1831-1918 <u>Sketch of the Early History of the African Methodist Episcopal Zion Church with Jubilee Souvenir And Appendix:</u> Electronic Edition © This work is the property of the University of North Carolina at Chapel Hill. It may be used freely by individuals (title page) Sketch of the Early History of the African Methodist Episcopal Zion Church with Jubilee Souvenir and an Appendix. p. 62

Bishop James Hoggard further discussed the split:

> When the first Methodist Episcopal (M.E.) Society (mainly white) was established in New York, among whom were several colored persons, the two races found no difficulty in the practice of religious fellowship and the equal enjoyment of religious rights and privileges; but as the Church grew in popularity and influence, prejudice of caste engendered Negro proscription. As colored members increased, race friction and proscription increased, which finally exhausted the patience of the colored members of the M.E. Society.[59]

This type of treatment, and the severely felt need for emancipation and religious freedom, was key among the underlying causes which thus prompted the founding members of the African Methodist Episcopal Zion Church to initially hold meetings among themselves.

Bishop Christopher Rush, "born 1777; ordained Deacon and Elder, July 23, 1822, Consecrated Bishop, May 18, 1826, Died July 16, 1873"[60], painted a different picture. If surly feelings existed, according to the account of he who lived through this period, they never surfaced. Books exist today which speak to the history of the African Methodist Episcopal Zion Church. The earliest written[61] of these was first published in 1843 and reprinted in 1866

---

[59] Bishop James Clinton Hoggard, the African Methodist Episcopal Zion Church, 197201996: a Bicentennial Commemorative History, (Charlotte, North Carolina: A.M.E. Zion Publishing House, 1998), 6.

[60] William J. Walls, The African Methodist Episcopal Zion Church: The Reality of the Black Church, (North Carolina: A.M.E. Zion Publishing House, 1974), p.566

[61] Christopher Rush George Collins. A Short Account of the Rise and Progress of the African Methodist Episcopal Church in America 1843. Republished by A.M.E. Zion Historical Society (Charlotte, North Carolina) 2000

and in 2000.

> At the beginning of our organization, Zion had the eminent George Collins recording the actions and deeds of the movement. He was a man of brilliance, a school teacher of his own race group. Because of the inadequacy of education for blacks in the age, he also had to earn his living by other trades. Therefore, in addition to the teaching, he was a painter and operated a grocery store on the side. George Collins in effect, was our first General Secretary. The committee of five,... Selected...George Collins to edit the first Discipline in 1820. He was an expert record keeper and zealous church worker, and amanuensis to Bishop Rush most of the Bishop's years of service. Unfortunately, the first church records were destroyed in a disastrous fire in 1839.[62]

It was with Collins' help that Rush expunges the theory that their break was acrimonious. Said Rush:

> In the year 1796, when the colored members of the Methodist Episcopal Church in the City of New York became increased, and feeling a desire for the privilege of holding meetings of their own, where they might have an opportunity to exercise their spiritual gifts among themselves, and thereby be more useful one to the other, a few of the most intelligent of our brethren obtained permission from Bishop Francis Asbury to hold meetings by themselves, in the intervals of the regular preaching hours of our white brethren, in the best manner they could. The names of some of the men who went forward in this dawning of religious privileges were Francis Jacobs, William Brown, Peter Williams, Abraham Thompson, June Scott, Samuel Pontier, Thomas Mill, James Varick, William Hamilton, and some others whose names are not now

---

62   William J. Walls, The African Methodist Episcopal Zion Church: The Reality of the Black Church, (North Carolina: A.M.E. Zion Publishing House, 1974), p. 267

recollected, who united together, and, by some means, hired a house on Cross Street, between Mulberry and Orange Streets, which formerly was a stable, but at that time was occupied by William Miller as a cabinetmakers shop...In this house, they held prayer meetings on Sunday afternoons, in the interval of Divine Service among our white brethren, between afternoon and evening or night service, and held also preaching and exhorting meetings on Wednesdays, by such of our colored brethren as were licensed to preach and exhort.[63]

Secretary/Editor of the Historical Society, African Methodist Episcopal Zion Church, Dr. James David Armstrong addressed the early beginnings of Zion Methodism, looking at its early formation and dating the conception as early as 1780 when the Blacks were placed in separate classes, contributing to the feelings associated with the repugnant caste system. It is widely understood that the Blacks were under the supervision of White leaders. As time went on, they met privately to discuss the possibility of being their own men and women, operating their own church, "for they realized that if they could have separate classes or societies, they could ultimately have a separate Church. They felt that they could conduct their own affairs, move in their own direction and care for their own needs."[64]

The men of Class 31 of John Street Methodist Episcopal Church were men of African descent under White leadership -- not unexpected given the situation of that day. It was hardly likely to find a class of mixed races in the church. History does not provide the names of the influential and intelligent

---

[63] Christopher Rush George Collins. A Short Account of the Rise and Progress of the African Methodist Episcopal Church in America 1843. Republished by A.M.E. Zion Historical Society (Charlotte, North Carolina 2000), p.4

[64] James David Armstrong, A Brief Historical Survey of the African Methodist Episcopal Zion Church (North Carolina: The A.M.E. Zion Historical Society 2004), 4

Blacks who met to choose the committee to seek a meeting with Bishop Francis Asbury of the Methodist Episcopal Church to seek permission to hold meetings by themselves, but it does posit the names of those commissioned and who successfully executed the task as Francis Jacobs, William Brown, Peter Williams and June Scott.

As Walls puts it: "from then on they moved with magnifying force, not only to produce some of the world's greatest freedom fighters and advocates, but to shine as a beacon light, for individual rights and privileges, in becoming prominent and well known as 'The Freedom Church.'"[65] Gaining permission to meet was however just the beginning of what was to prove a long journey with many bumps in the road to autonomy. The next step, ascertaining a place of worship, was a group effort spearheaded by "Francis Jacobs, William Brown, Peter Williams, Abraham Thompson, June Scott, Samuel Pontier, Thomas Miller, James Varick and William Hamilton."[66]

It is reported that finding such a place was accomplished with much difficulty; notwithstanding, highly symbolic is the fact that the first meeting home of the nucleus of the denomination was a house on *Cross* Street which had formerly been an old stable and at that time being used as a cabinet shop by William Miller, an exhorter. Seemingly, like the Jesus they had placed so much faith in, there was no room for them but the stable, and the cross He died on as well as the many they had to bear as a people, could not be forgotten nor would they lose hope.

---

65   Ibid. 45.
66   Bishop John Jamison Moore, History of the A.M.E Zion Church in America (Charlotte, North Carolina: The A.M.E. Zion Historical Society, 2004), p. 5

In their midst God had already provided three licensed local preachers --along with the exhorter Miller -- Abraham Thompson, June Scott and Thomas Miller. The White preachers continued to conduct services on Sundays, but this group, along with the help of other Black preachers, conducted prayer and other meetings.

It is evident that from its inception, the African Methodist Episcopal Zion Church was called to be a liberator and bring its people to a state of autonomy and self-sufficiency. If this were not so, its founders could well have remained members of John Street Methodist Episcopal Church and tolerate a racist, segregationist and dehumanizing existence. Cross Street provided them a taste of the joys which came of unbridled worship and a vision of what could yet be achieved. Any wonder that the next step in the process of the birth of the denomination was to wholly withdraw from the Methodist Episcopal Church, erect their own church building and form themselves into a corporate body autonomous from John Street. Jesus was crucified and rose on the third day. Unwittingly, the group maintained the symbolism for it was three years before they again imposed on the intellect of the most respected religious leaders of their congregation on the best way to move forward. As the decisions revealed, the fathers and mothers of this denomination had no problem whatsoever with Methodism per se and even adopted the entire Methodist Episcopal polity, hymns and Articles of Religion.

It is interesting to compare the Methodist Articles with those of the Episcopal Church. The extra-canonical books, known as the Apocrypha, are given a higher status in the Episcopal Church than in the Methodist traditions;

the descent of Christ into Hell and the article on the creeds are omitted; there is less emphasis on the damnation of those because of original sin; and a sense that work done before salvation is obviously sinful. In short, the Methodist traditions are more Protestant and less traditionally Catholic. The African Methodist Episcopal Zion Church is a descendent of the Methodist tradition in so many ways. It is of great importance that the breakaway church even took the name Methodist Episcopal, merely adding 'African' to its name to differentiate and underscore its branch of Methodism. History provides the names of six of the nine trustees appointed to the various facets of the undertaking: Francis Jacobs, William Brown, Thomas Miller, George Collins, Peter Williams, Thomas Sipkins, William Hamilton and George Collins. Francis Jacobs was appointed Chairman of the Board of Trustees; Thomas Miller, Treasurer, and George Collins Secretary. After some disappointment in their efforts towards procurement of land, they

> obtained two lots of ground, each twenty-five feet front and seventy-five feet deep, situate at the corner of Church and Leonard Streets, and fronting on Church Street, which circumstance renewed the courage of the Trustees who agreed to accept the said ground, and resolved upon its being a suitable place for the contemplated building...They therefore went with their subscription books, and solicited the public generally for aid in this great and laudable work, for the benefit of coloured people, in the city of New York, and in the month of September, or October, of the year 1800, they effected a framed building, on the aforesaid spot of ground, thirty-five feet wide and forty-five long, which was dedicated for the House of God.[67]

---

67   Christopher Rush, <u>A Short Account of the Rise and Progress of the African Methodist Episcopal Church in America</u> (21 Grand Street, New York: W. Marks, 1843), pp. 12-13.

The Blacks continued their relationship with the Methodist Episcopal Church – that of the White Elder preaching on Sunday afternoons except when communion was being served, usually on the second Sunday of each month and in the morning. Meanwhile, at all other services – Wednesdays, Fridays, other times on Sundays, the Black local preachers took charge. And so for a period, the old ship of Zion sailed smoothly along these waters. It was only for a period however, for the annals of history reveal that there was great disagreement within as well as without. First noted was the break by preachers Abraham Thompson and June Scott who later returned to the fold with some of the members who had accompanied them when they linked up with John Edwards (who had been expelled from the Friends Society) to form the Union Society. Edwards used a new house of worship with a parsonage as bait. The next split came with the departure of Thomas Sipkins who seemingly wanted to be in charge and was dismissed due to insubordination. He managed to persuade William Miller, then a deacon, to leave the Zion church and together they formed the Asbury Church, drawing from the Zion membership as well. Among those who went with them was William Lambert, who later went to Philadelphia and joined the Black Methodists in that city, at the Bethel Church. Moore states that "having obtained license from the Bishop, as a kind of Missionary Preacher, he returned to New York, and being denied the use of the Pulpit in Asbury Church, he determined to raise a church or congregation for Bishop Allen's connection."[68] Therein lay the beginnings of actions and reactions that led to strained relations between Zion and Bethel Methodism. I strongly regret that I could not find material on the split from the African Methodist Episcopal Church's point of

---

68   Bishop John Jamison Moore, <u>History of the A.M.E Zion Church in America</u> (Charlotte, North Carolina: The A.M.E. Zion Historical Society, 2004), p. 35

view. Moore puts it thusly:

> The church (Bethel) was dedicated on Sunday, the 23rd day of July, 1820, shortly after which Rev. Richard Allen himself, arrived in New York, and sanctioned all that had been done by those men acting under his supervision. Thus he laid the foundation of a connectional strife that has been perpetuated against Zion Connection by the Bethel Church to this day. Had Bishop Allen and his followers pursued a different course at this time, as the leader of his body, there is no doubt that Zion and Bethel Connections would have been one body today."[69]

Notwithstanding, the record is clear that members of the African Methodist Episcopal Zion Church visited and participated, going out of their way to maintain a pleasant working relationship between the two denominations. Displaying the subtlety, diplomacy and the intellect which he would need to undergird his leadership skill, James Varick, who would be elected the first Bishop in Zion, was not afraid to stand with Bishop Allen and preached on this occasion. Indeed, it was his actions that led to a working relationship between the groups.

As time passed the struggles continued. Zion's leadership had to move with haste to change course when the White pastor presiding over the Zion and Asbury churches notified them that he and a great portion of White members had withdrawn from the White Methodist Episcopal Church. Among the several reasons he disclosed, none froze the blood of his congregation and spurred them to further prayer and action than the fact that their General Conference had passed a resolution seeking to gain from the State of New York

69 Ibid., p.18.

incorporation papers which would give preachers power over the assets of the churches under their governance. Dealing with continued racial insults and the need to 'go along to get along' was one thing; losing control of all they had sacrificed for was another all together. The leaders met with their members. In an effort to clear the thinking on what path to take, going back to the White church as well as joining Bishop Allen were considered. The congregation agreed that neither was palatable; free worship was the only feasible next step.

Words from present-day Zion scholar Dr. Reginald Broadnax provide insight into this area as he writes: "the discrimination faced by Zion did not occur in John Street Church, but in the broader M.E. Church, in reference to the advancement and ordination of Zion's preachers. Subsequently, any claim that Zion was discriminated against within John Street Church is a misrepresentation of Zion's history."[70] In our major history book in use, written by Walls, John Street continues to be blamed and the history unintentionally distorted.

It was a slow and painstaking process from the time of withdrawal to the date the African Methodist Episcopal Zion Church was organized; 1796-1822. However, several meetings later, the official members appointed James Varick, George Collins, Charles Anderson, Christopher Rush and William Miller to form a Discipline. As a result, down through the ages, the Founders' Address has always been included in the first pages of the Church's Book of Discipline, from which I quote:

---

70 Reginald David Broadnax, Ph. D. The Organization of The African Methodist Episcopal Zion Church And Its Contribution To Both Methodist Polity and Methodist Episcopacy" in <u>The A.M.E. Zion Quarterly Review</u> (Charlotte, North Carolina: A.M.E. Zion Publishing House, OctOber 2006), p.14

Beloved Brethren: We think it proper to state briefly that after due consideration, the official members of The African Methodist Episcopal Zion...Churches in the City of New York have been led to conclude that such was the relation in which we stood to the white Bishops and Conference, relative to the ecclesiastical government of the African Methodist Church or Society in America, so long as we remain in that situation our Preachers would never be able to enjoy those privileges which the Discipline of the white Church holds out to all its Members that are called to preach, in consequence, of the limited access our brethren had to those privileges, and particularly in consequence of the difference of color. We have been led also to conclude that usefulness of our Preachers have been very much hindered, and our brethren in general have been deprived of those blessings which almighty God may have designed to grant them, through the means of those Preachers whom He has from time to time raised up from among them, because there has been no means adopted by the said Bishop and conference for our Preachers to travel through the connection and promulgate the Gospel of our Lord Jesus Christ...[71]

The address identifies the denomination as The African Methodist Episcopal Zion Church, but its name at the time of organization was The African Methodist Episcopal Church. The first church built at Church and Leonard streets was called Zion. A number of reasons no doubt led to the change, but oral tradition emphasizes the rancor, acrimony and animosity between the Bethel-ites and Bishop Allen. Given that difficult relationship, there was need to differentiate between The African Methodist Church started

---

[71] The Book of Discipline of The African Methodist Episcopal Zion Church 2004, (Charlotte, North Carolina: A.M.E. Zion Publishing House, 2005) iii.

in Philadelphia in 1778 and The African Methodist Church started in New York in 1796. Thus, to establish and allow all to differentiate between these two groups, "Zion was finally incorporated as a part of the legal title"[72].

How does one describe freedom and equality? Even in the twentieth and twenty-first centuries the question does resound:

> Freedom, what is it? It is not license to do as one pleases; it is not the privilege to oppress; to persecute or to infringe upon the rights of another. Freedom is God's gift to man. It is a gift of liberty, equality and fraternity. Liberty does not mean that you can do as you please. It is the free unencumbered and responsible fellowship of (humanity). By equality, we do not mean that every man is born with the same capacity and intelligence. Equality has to do with justice and fair play. It is equal opportunity to live, grow and contribute to human society. [73]

What or who influenced the leaders of the African Methodist Episcopal Zion Church? Who could they pattern themselves after? Massa was certainly a very poor example. One is led to believe that while they could and probably did to some extent look upon the leadership of the Methodist Episcopal Church for how to do things the Methodist way, innate wisdom resulted in them singing, providing music, praying and preaching in ways that came naturally to those of African heritage.

The first Bishop elected in the African Methodist Episcopal Zion Church was one of those who led the group out of John Street Methodist

---

72   Bishop J.W. Hood, <u>One Hundred Years of the African Methodist Episcopal Zion Church: The Centennial of African Methodism</u> (New York: A.M.E. Zion Book Concern, 1895), p57.
73   Ruben L. Speaks, <u>The Minister and His Task,</u> (Charlotte, North Carolina: A.M.E. Zion Publishing House, 1970), 75-76.

Episcopal Church: James Varick. Varick, of revered memory, was born in Newburgh, New York. Historians state that Varick was born some 50 years after John Wesley, June 17, 1750. His father is recorded as Richard Varick, his mother an unnamed slave or former slave of the Varicks', a Dutch family. Having led the exodus from John Street, James Varick, a father of seven who was married to Aurelia Jones in 1790, was ordained a Deacon May 18, 1806, an Elder June 22, 1821 and was consecrated one year later, July 22, 1822.

A shoemaker by trade, Varick died on July 21, 1827 and his remains are buried in a crypt beneath the sanctuary of the Mother African Methodist Episcopal Zion Church in New York. Many names have been used to describe him; teacher, advocate, preacher are but three more in regard to his position with A.M.E. Zion. The African Methodist Episcopal Zion Church (Freedom Church as it is still known today) brought freedom to those of African descent since the church was established to be and has, through the ages, been controlled by descendants of the African race, but in the interest of humanity, regardless of race, color, sex or condition. The modern Zion Denomination includes over 2,700 churches with some two million, plus members in the United States, the Virgin Islands, Africa, India, England, the Caribbean and South America.

Today, the denomination maintains a cadre of twelve Presiding Bishops, and four retired Bishops, the last Bishop being elected in 2008, the ninety-eighth of her kind. Within the last quarter of a century, female ministers have offered themselves for election to the Episcopacy, the Class of 2008 consecrating the denomination's first female Bishop.

From its lowly beginnings, this church is now experiencing growth on the continent of Africa, in India, England, the Caribbean, South America and the United States. The twelve Bishops of the Church preside over Conferences separated into Districts and, with fervor and passion, provide leadership in the spiritual, socio-economic, ecumenical and religious life of the denomination.

In its beginnings, leadership in the Church was not merely relegated to preaching, for especially in that era, there were blatant and gross uncertainties, and even within the group, differences of opinion were rife. Indeed, even today questions still swirl in some areas of the Church as to how and why the denomination came into being. There are some tales of the knights in shining armor that rose up and fought against the evils of the day, slew the dragons and brought the race out to worship safely and freely. Others hold that this was not the case at all.

No one explained any of this to the founding fathers so how did they make it in leadership and administration? What accounts for this Church led by a diverse group of Blacks to be in existence till now?

CHAPTER THREE
BISHOPS, LEADERSHIP
AND THE AFRICAN METHODIST
EPISCOPAL ZION CHURCH

The African Methodist Episcopal Zion Church employs an Episcopal form of government. Twelve bishops actively supported by retired bishops provide the top administrative and spiritual leadership of the entire denomination and as a body they are referred to as the Board of Bishops. The Board has general oversight, deals with promotion of the Church and ensures that its mission and polity for its 1.2 million members remains true to the message of its founding fathers. By regularly scheduled meetings this Board of twelve elected church leaders keeps the "Ole Ship of Zion" afloat.

The most senior Bishop is so identified by his years of service, but presidency of the Board rotates on a six-month basis with each Bishop serving in that capacity while carrying on his episcopal responsibilities.

The authority of the Bishop is discussed in the Book of Discipline, a library of laws, policies and regulations promulgated at each quadrennial conference of the church and while each leader of the church espouses a different leadership style over her conference, she must be careful in her zeal not to abrogate the Discipline. This structure has sustained Methodism and Zion Methodism in particular, for over two centuries and had initially commissioned a cadre of intelligent but mostly unlettered men to evangelize. This assemblage has, over the years, continued to be highly respected, and grown to be a learned and significant segment of lettered men and women who have gone forth to spread the Gospel and win souls for God's kingdom.

The African Methodist Episcopal Zion denomination is a Connectional Church. This is explained very clearly by Bishop Walls when he writes:

> When I was a boy, I was taught that ours was not to be called a denomination, but a connection. The word "denomination" meant Methodist, and the African Methodist Episcopal Zion Church was a Methodist Connection or a Connection of the Methodist Church system. This has a two-way meaning: it means connection with other Methodist churches but separate; and second, it means connection with each other as congregations with a central form of church policy, governing each congregation, while each congregation maintains a separate and distinctive identity.[74]

This tradition sees itself not as a separate denomination, but rather a church with deep connections of history and theology with the tradition of Methodism. Now the conception of connection is reflected in its own understanding of success. The success of the work in the church is seen at two levels – its interconnectedness and the team approach (more clearly visible within the Episcopal Districts). Each Bishop appoints Presiding Elders, Pastors, Ministers and Lay leaders, all continuously serving to foster the mission of the denomination in order to "advance the Church of Jesus Christ, and safe guard the glorious heritage bequeathed us by our forefathers, preserve our tradition as

---

74   Bishop William Walls, 'The Place of the Negro Church in History' in Bishop William Walls, <u>Connectionalism and the Negro Church.</u> (private papers,1954) pp. 11.

a people called "Zion Methodist", maintain Christian fellowship and discipline, edify believers, convert the world, transform society, and perfect our unity and structure."[75] At the denominational[76] level, in the period between general conferences, there are Administrative Boards of equal representation of lay and clergy from each Episcopal District along with Bishops (three on each Board). Unlike the situation with Jesus and His disciples, this team approach has much more organizational structure, no doubt necessitated by the numerical strength and large geographical area the churches cover.

Especially in the late eighteenth century and through the mid nineteenth century, education for Blacks, including Black clergy, was not widely available. College education was for a long time a luxury, but it is commendable that a few of them took opportunities in academia, studied to show themselves improved, and worked amongst their people. What is amazing is that disparate groups within the fold focused solely on the establishment of a church where they could worship, since that mattered most to each of them. More pressing than any of their differences was their gratitude to the living God and their innate desire to praise and worship Him without restrictions. They truly believed it was their faith and belief in the redemptive and saving power of God which sustained them.

"Leadership," according to well-known author and leadership expert Dr. John Maxwell, "develops daily"[77], not in a day, and, the scholar further posits, "everything rises and falls on leadership."[78] The three bishops under review were

---

75 The Book of Discipline of The African Methodist Episcopal Zion Church 2004 p. 2
76 Having just explained that it is not a denomination, I will now for ease of reference describe the church as a denomination, but do while recognizing that this is understood in a distinctive way.
77 John C. Maxwell. The 21 Indispensable Qualities of a Leader: Becoming the Person Others Will Want to Follow. (Nashville: Thomas Nelson Publishers, 1999), p. x
78 Ibid. p. xi

certainly ahead of their time, for in administration of their conferences--with thousands under their charge and many churches--they quite clearly exercised the kind of progressive leadership--economic and spiritual--that kept Blacks and their churches in a viable state of progressive development and expansion.

How did these men of the cloth, with a steady hand, sound judgment, armed with Bible and Discipline, but void of modern day leadership theories move this Zion to such a colossal level? Was it not the hand of God on this denomination at this time and was it not the fervor of these Christian giants that propelled this "Ole Ship" through what must have been difficult waters?

If the apostles today were asked to name the qualities they thought most necessary to qualify one to be a leader, Acts 6:3 would no doubt provide the answer: "Therefore, brethren, seek out from among you seven men of good reputation, full of the Holy Spirit and wisdom' whom we may appoint over this business." In one verse, we are brought face-to-face with leadership qualities and theories from one of the oldest texts of the ages --the Good Book. Many a theologian and writer can be quoted in this instance, but I was particularly interested to see how John C. Maxwell, eminent author and leadership expert had addressed this issue and portion of scripture. In so doing he said:[79]

> ABCs of Leadership: Leaders Must Be Selected and Developed. Good leadership responds effectively to the need for more leaders and workers. Apparently, no one took a vote to determine the identity of these people. The leaders were chosen. The leadership of the early church practiced the ABCs OF LEADERSHIP. They:

Attracted leaders
Believed in them
Chose them

---
[79] Tim Elmore. The Maxwell Leadership Bible. (NKJV) Revised and Updated. (Nashville: Thomas Nelson;2007), 1352

Developed them.

The apostles had specific qualifications in mind for the leaders they wanted, and chose men who were:

a) known from their sphere of influence..."seek out from among you."
b) people who could serve on a team - "seven men."
c) trusted among the people - "of goods reputation."
d) Empowered for the task - "full of the Holy Spirit."
5) competent and intelligent - "full of wisdom."
6) responsible - "whom we may appoint over this business."

Dr. Kenneth Q. James[80], a modern-day scholar of the African Methodist Episcopal Zion Church, clearly points out what the founding fathers knew first hand -- leadership is not only about title or position or labels; leadership ability does not only come from our perceived or imagined strengths but also from our mastering and acknowledging our weaknesses and with God's help, conquering or managing them. Oral tradition strongly avers that Walls, Spottswood and Shaw subscribed to the belief that to improve the governance of the church is not to find perfect men and women but to find the imperfect who are willing to acknowledge their imperfections to the perfect God and allow Him to work through and with them. Walls (see Appendix One) was known to assist young pastors early in their careers as he pointed to areas in their ministry that needed attention.

Thomas Edward Frank, Associate Professor of Church Administration and Congregational Life at Candler School of Theology speaks to the need for identifying leadership styles that appeal and support the needs of a denomination. Said he:

Churches face enormous institutional challenges at the

80   Kenneth Q. James. Another Look At Leadership

beginning of the twenty-first century. Particularly among those denominations that have been in ministry and mission for generations and have built hundreds of congregational facilities, schools and colleges, hospitals and homes, simply maintaining their institutional infrastructure and existing ministries is daunting enough. The further challenge of enhancing their strengths and commitments through a growing membership, all in the midst of the immense social changes of recent decades, would seem to require no less than significant transformation... Social and cultural changes that have swept across the US over the past fifty years have created enormous anxiety about the continuing place of churches in the larger culture. Many authors have warned that the churches must adjust to living in an entirely new post-Christendom era that a "new paradigm" of church and society is emerging and that taken for granted worlds of assumptions are passing from the scene.[81]

The African Methodist Episcopal Zion Church is no different. Indeed, it has made it clear that while understanding human behavior and being able to relate to people is important, assisting pastors to develop good leadership and management styles which reflect their theology is vital. The leaders, both lay and clergy must perforce realize that they leave their mark which, consciously and unconsciously, influence those with whom they work and those whom they lead. In like manner, individuals themselves emulate the behavior and leadership styles of those who in their estimation are successful, those they like or admire.

It was Maxwell[82] who posed the questions: "What makes people want

---

81   Thomas Edward Frank: The Discourse Of Leadership and the Practice of Administration Emory University, Atlanta, Georgia. http://www.christianleadrs.org/JRL/Spring 2002/Discourse, p.1

82   John C. Maxwell The 21 Indispensable Qualities of a Leader: Becoming the Person Others will want to follow. (Nashville, Tennessee: Thomas Nelson, Inc, 1999), p. ix

to follow a leader? Why do people reluctantly comply with one leader while passionately following another to the ends of the earth as was the case of the 1978 massacre of Rev. Jim Jones and his followers in Guyana, what makes a difference in peoples' leadership in the real world?"[83] Henry Richard Blackaby provided the answer in addressing 'The Leader's Challenge' in their book on Spiritual Leadership.

> Christian leaders who know God and who know how to lead in a Christian manner will be phenomenally more effective in their world than even the most skilled and qualified leaders who lead without God....The challenge for today's leaders is to discern the difference between the latest leadership fads and timeless truths established by God. [84]

This dictum tells us that Episcopal leaders must be circumspect in their behavior and grounded in sound theology.

McAlpine addressed this issue when he dealt with one serving God for the right motive and not being a people pleaser:

> Just like Jesus, Paul sought no glory for himself. His great desire which he expressed to the church at Philippi was that Christ... be magnified in my Body, whether by life or by death... (He) was not interested in the approval of people; he was interested in God's approval...Like Jesus Paul preached truth even though on many occasions it did not please people"[85]

Like Paul, this is largely the legacy of the subjects of this study.

---

83 Ibid.
84 Henry Richard Blackaby. Spiritual Leadership: Moving People on to God's Agenda. (Nashville, Tennessee: Broadman Holman Publishers,2001), p. 14
85 John C. Maxwell The 21 Indispensable Qualities of a Leader: Becoming the Person others will want to follow. (Nashville, Tennessee: Thomas Nelson, Inc, 1999), p. 102

Efrain Agosto, Professor of New Testament, in his book Servant Leadership: Jesus and Paul, says "Leaders have followers, but more than that they guide those who would follow toward new and challenging paths."[86] With this thought the writer's mind went directly to the three Bishops, men of God who also happen to be most often noted in daily discourse of ministers today: Bishop Herbert Bell Shaw, Bishop Stephen Gill Spottswood and Bishop William Jacob Walls. Each of these stalwart church leaders has left an indelible imprint on the life of the African Methodist Episcopal Zion Church in completely different ways. All have earned to a greater or lesser degree the moniker of 'freedom fighter' and all have, in their own way, contributed to the expansion of the numbers or borders of this great Church, and today it showers praise on them.

This gives the history upon which the African Methodist Episcopal Zion Church stands. As it did then, it now provides meaning, a purpose and a portrait that resonates within the heart and soul of the descendants of Black mothers and fathers, of a God who makes a way out of nowhere, liberating His Black people who are oppressed by others, oppressed by a system which continues to enslave them one hundred and forty-eight years after emancipation and which causes some to further enslave themselves in many ways.

There is even a new radical movement on the scene, whose aim seems to be removing the church from its historical position in the lives of Blacks.

> the after effects of Reconstruction called the Black church forth as the community's sole institution of power whether urban or rural, the Black church was the only institution totally

---
[86] Efrain Agosto. <u>Servant Leadership: Jesus Paul</u>. (St. Louis, Missouri: Chalice Press, 2005), p. 6

controlled by Black people. It was the only place outside the home where Blacks could express themselves freely and take independent action. The church community was the heart, center, and basic organization of Black life. And those who were religious leaders searched the Scriptures to vie distinctive shapes and patterns to the words, ideas that the Black community used to speak about God and God's relationship to an oppressed people. [87]

---

[87] Katie G. Cannon. Katie's Canon: Womanism and the Soul of the Black Community. (New York: Continuum Publishing, 1995), p,51

CHAPTER FOUR

BISHOP WILLIAM JACOB WALLS: THE IMPACT OF HIS LIFE, LEADERSHIP AND LEGACY ON THE AFRICAN METHODIST EPISCOPAL ZION CHURCH

A cursory internet search suggests that "Chimney Rock is the natural fulfillment of your trip to the North Carolina Mountains...the perfect place to reconnect with nature and spend time with family and friends."[88] It was in Chimney Rock that William Walls was born -- in the Blue Hill Mountains of Rutherford County, North Carolina, Friday, May 8, 1885.

The records become a bit fuzzy here, an unfortunate truth which only serves to underscore the need for good archival sources. However, pulling from several oral and some varied re-printed sources, we understand that his father died before the family moved to live with Walls' maternal grandparents in Asheville, North Carolina. Meanwhile, Reverence of a Senior Bishop[89] claims he had moved to Asheville from as early as two years:

> When he was two years old, his family moved to Asheville where they lived with his maternal grandparents, Mr. and Mrs. John Flack. Thus, his childhood life centered on this city. He

---

[88] www.chimneyrockpark.com
[89] Ibid.

was of poor surrounds, which made it necessary for both his mother and father to work while he was raised in the home of his grandparents.

After his father's death, Walls had to assume the mantle of responsibility, doing deliveries, chores, and working as a house boy, and yard keeper. Doing so, he earned enough to help his mother sustain the family.

Walls was a student of a private school on the west side of Asheville for one year and afterward

> attended Allen Industrial School of Asheville, N.C.; transferred to Livingstone College, and completed the grammar and normal schools, (funded in part by his local church). He received a B.A., from Livingstone College, 1908, a B.D. from Hood Theological Seminary, 1913, studied journalism and philosophy at Columbia University, 1921-22, and received his M.A. in Christian Education, University of Chicago, 1941.[90]

It is said that as a boy he loved to study and that his dream was to be a preacher. Oral tradition has it that "with trees for the pillars of his temple and birds for his audience, young Walls preached his trial sermons"[91] in the hills of Asheville. There is little doubt that his preaching fervor and regular attendance at all the Sunday schools in his area, his love for reading and, above all, his sincerity of purpose and love for knowledge did not escape his mother with whom he had a close relationship, nor indeed, the members of Hopkins

---

90   William J. Walls, <u>The African Methodist Episcopal Zion Church: Reality of the Black Church</u> (Charlotte, North Carolina: A.M.E. Zion Publishing House, 1974), 600
91   <u>The Star of Zion</u>, Vol. 70 (Charlotte, North Carolina) p. 7

Chapel, his home church, and the residents of the hamlet. Mother redoubled her efforts, but the laundry where she worked did not pay enough to send him to school. If it were at all possible to redouble a redouble, she did it; she did all she physically could, making every effort to earn as much as she could, never ceasing to encourage and to push him to work hard and complete what chores he had to do, but more so, to strive for excellence in his studies and religious growth and development. His efforts coupled with her ardent prayers and faith in a God who could make a way out of nowhere resulted in his receiving a scholarship from his local church.

Walls, who dreamed of being a preacher, oft preached in the mountains to the trees and birds, but little realized how quickly his dreams would become a reality when, at the age of 14, he would stand before a packed congregation in his home church and preach his trial sermon. Thus, on Sunday, September 10, 1899, Asheville, N.C. was privileged to witness the humble beginnings of a boy evangelist.

Licensed to preach in 1899, William Jacob Walls "joined the Blue Ridge Conference at Johnson City, Tenn. October 6, 1902."[92] On Tuesday, October 20, 1903 he was ordained by Bishop C.R. Harris and roughly two years later, during Bishop Harris' illness, Bishop J. W. Smith assisted in his ordination to the eldership on Friday, October, 16, 1905[93]: "He pastored the Cedar Grove Circuit, Cleveland, N.C. 1904-1906, Landis and Milers Chapel Circuit; 1906-1907 Lincolnton, N.C., Soldier's Memorial, Salisbury, N.C. 1910-1913." Walls went on to pastor one of the key pulpits of Zion in Louisville, Kentucky where

---

92   William J. Walls, <u>The African Methodist Episcopal Zion Church: Reality of the Black Church</u> (Charlotte, North Carolina: A.M.E. Zion Publishing House, 1974), 600
93   <u>A.M.E. Zion Sesquicentennial Lecte…….</u> (N.Y. Conf.: 1821-1971),p. 917

he built a new edifice which stands even today. It was Speaks who in his book, *The Minister and His Task*, said:

> During the Dark Ages when the Roman Empire had fallen and Christian society was in a chaotic state, it was the great centers of learning that kept aglow the flickering light of free thought and scientific inquiry. Because it served as a preserver of Christian ideals and Christian culture, these institutions became a hot bed for the Renaissance and the Reformation. They were the fountain head from which sprang the great streams of reformed doctrine and policy. In this age of secularist materialism, communistic atheism, and fascistic racialism, it is the duty of the Church related school to preserve our Christian heritage; to keep aglow the flickering flame of Christian idealism, democratic individualism, and Christianized socialism. We must pass on to our posterity the essence of our Judeo Christian-Hellenistic culture.[94]

William Jacob Walls was one who unwittingly has passed on to his posterity the essence of our culture.

EDITOR, STAR OF ZION

Walls was elected editor of the Star of Zion in 1920 and served until 1924 when he was elected bishop. After 44 active years in the episcopacy, he retired in 1968 and was commissioned Historiographer by the General Conference, to construct, edit, and publish a "comprehensive history of the denomination."[95] The obituary of Bishop William Jacob Walls chronicles him as stately, magnanimous, sterling and visionary as they extol the legacy of

---

94   Ruben L. Speaks. The Minister and His Task. (Charlotte, North Carolina: A.M.E. Zion Publishing House, 1970), p. 77
95   William J. Walls, The African Methodist Episcopal Zion Church: Reality of the Black Church (Charlotte, North Carolina: A.M.E. Zion Publishing House, 1974), 600

leadership he has left behind. Never had so much been wrapped up in so small a dash.

While serving as Editor of The Star of Zion, the denominational weekly publication from 1920 to 1924, Wall placed the paper on "the largest exchange list in its history"[96] with the leading religious journals of the day and tripled its circulation from 3,000 to 9,000. In 1991 the circulation was 8,200 every Thursday. Today, the circulation of this publication has moved to 18,000 once per month.[97] The Star of Zion was among the many to salute this bishop on the occasion of his sixtieth birthday. Said one article:

> In paying this tribute to the genius and labor of Bishop William Jacob Walls we feel a peculiar interest because he is the only living former editor of the Star of Zion. And we utter only what everyone knows when we say that he was one of the best editors the paper has ever had. His connection with, and interest in, the Star of Zion has probably actuated him in many a kindly gesture to those who have followed in his footsteps.... Bishop Walls' extraordinary intellect, his broad training together with his amazing zeal and capacity for knowledge has made him one of the best informed churchmen in the world today. His marvelous energy, expending itself in the most extraordinary, painstaking detail in his labor, and his matchless captivating oratory render him one of the most influential personalities on the American scene in our generation...No man ever fought harder for purity and uprightness in the ranks of the ministry than Bishop Walls and yet nowhere in Christendom will there be found a man with greater tolerance and a finer spirit of forgiveness than he. He is a firm advocate of discipline and devotion to the tenets of the church.[98]

---

96 Ibid,p351.
97 Office of the Star of Zion
98 The Star Of Zion (Charlotte, North Carolina Thursday, September 30, 1943) p. 4ff

TELLING A NEGLECTED STORY

Reverend William J. Walls was elevated to the rank of the episcopacy in 1924 and served as Chairman, Board of Religious Education and Board of Publications, A.M.E. Zion Church; Treasurer, Fraternal Council of Negro Churches; Trustee, United International Christian Endeavor Society; Chairman, Livingstone College Trustee Board; Trustee, Gammon Theological Seminary; Chaplain and member of the Negro Business League; and member of International Council of Religious Education, National Association for the Advancement of Colored People, World Sunday School Association, National Commission of Relations of Young Men Christian Association, Phi Beta Sigma, Masons, Odd Fellows, Knights of Pythians, Elks, Urban League, Chicago Council of Negro Organizations, and the Executive Committee of the Federal Council of Churches of Christ in America. He was in 1946 the Chairman of the A.M.E. Zion Sesquicentennial Celebration General Committee, Commissioner of the National Protestant Study Conference on "Just and Durable Peace" at Cleveland, and was selected by the Fraternal Council of Churches to visit soldiers in foreign military zones at the request of the war department and the President.

Reverend Walls served as Fraternal Messenger to the Methodist Episcopal Church South General Conference in Atlantic, 1918, and to the Methodist Episcopal Church General Conference in Kansas City (by then he had been elected Bishop) in 1928. He was delegate to the ecumenical Methodist Conference in London in 1921 and in Atlanta in 1913, and while abroad he toured Belgium, France, Italy, Switzerland, Scandinavia, Finland, Poland and Germany.

FREEDOM FIGHTER/LIBERATOR

William Jacob Walls was a young man, thirty nine years of age, and still a novice Bishop, but there was little doubt that he clearly understood the need for liberation of the oppressed and was a freedom fighter in every sense of the word. Thus it was, this freedom fighter did not miss a beat when thrust into a fighting situation at the Union Railroad Terminal in Washington D.C.

> Recalling the conditions of the time, Walls explained that:
> The resurgence of the Ku Klux Klan influence, racial hatred, open lawlessness and the most notorious race riots of the nation's history after the war, produced a current of general unrest among the race. It began to appear to some Negroes that decisive and heroic measures should be taken to change the trend of worsening conditions nearly six decades after Emancipation.[99]

Twenty seven years later, he would still be preaching the gospel and rallying the National Fraternal Council of Churches to prayer and action. Referring to the assassination of a young black man, Harry T. Moore and his wife, Walls said to the group that

> the blow to that family is a blow to every black man and his family in America. Nay, more, it is a blow to every man and his family, for brutality and crime, once it is condoned, will know no color, nor creed and nor section...nor do I forget that the major hope and duty of the church is to work with one

---

[99] Bishop William J. Walls. <u>The African Methodist Episcopal Zion church: Reality of the Black Church.</u> (Charlotte, North Carolina: A.M.E. Zion Publishing House, 1974), p. 518

accord, not in separate camps with mountain walls between us, and men having spiritual and social wars. Wherever the spirit of the Lord is, there are not walls of separation. [100]

How sad that records (to date) do not contain the speeches, sermons and addresses of his first years as bishop.

Such was the mood of the country, and such was the plight of Blacks. It is no wonder that the Universal Negro Improvement Association established by Marcus Garvey in New York City grew rapidly and became a most powerful umbrella organization for black solidarity. Yet Garvey, a native of Jamaica, was deported, and his movement suppressed, but it had merely served to awaken the sleeping giant called the conscience of the Black man.

In 1925, one year after being elected to the episcopacy, he and the wife of a fellow Bishop, Mrs. Alleyne, refused to sit in the rear of the dining room of Union Station, Washington, DC and were refused service as a result. Indeed, they would have been served, had they been cooperative Negroes and sat in the rear. The two did not only refuse to sit in the rear but refused to leave. What resulted was a three hour sit-in which, from all reports, led to the end of segregation at this station.

In a day when it was unheard of, they stood firm and in spite of wide spread publicity, refused to yield, refused to budge an inch. Thus, thirty-odd years before Martin Luther King, Jr. began to lead groups in passive resistance these two led a three-hour sit-in which history records resulted in the end of segregation in Union Station. His understanding of the scripture and efforts

---

[100] Annual Address to the Annual Convention of National Fraternal Council of Churches. "Our Day Smiting A Passage through a World Like this" (Atlanta Georgia: Wheat Street Baptist Church: April 3-4, 1953), p. 21

to give "distinctive shape and patterns to the words and ideas that the Black community used to speak about God and God's relationship to an oppressed people"[101] is reflected in the fact that during his tenure as a Bishop in the New York conference the number of churches almost doubled.

Zion's historian for a number of years, Walls told the story in his own words. Said he:

> In pursuit of full rights continuously sought by the A.M.E. Zion Church, one of its bishops late encountered a shocking experience. In the East, every state south of Pennsylvania practiced Jim Crowism by approval or legality, except, as the world little believed, the public spot in the nation's capital—Union Railroad Terminal, through which thousands of passengers of all walks of life embarked and disembarked from around the world.
>
> On the morning of September 26, 1925, Bishop W.J. Walls, and the wife of his Episcopal classmate, Mrs. Lucille Alleyne, entered the dining room of Union Station and took their seats to be served, after the bishop had debarked a train from the South en route to Boston. They were told to go sit in the rear of the dining room, and when they refused to move, the waiters refused to serve them. The bishop and his guest staged a three hour sit-in, missing several connecting trains to Boston. When the bishop appealed to authorities and they refused to respond, he remonstrated and called for officers of the local National Association for the Advancement of Colored People who sent the president, Neval H. Thomas, with a delegation. Bishop E.D.W. Jones and Mr. William O. Walker, (then editor of the Washington Tribune), came to the scene. Representatives of the Civil Rights committee of Standard Oil Company and Bishop Walls insisted on being served on equal terms, and after undue humiliation in

---

101   Ibid.

desegregation of restaurants in the Washington, D.C. area. He returned from Boston a week afterward, and engaged in conferences with the same civil rights committees and the manager of the Washington Terminal Company, who ordered that segregation in that dining room be discontinued, which was done permanently."[102]

It was this man of action yet of passive resistance who was able to make a tiny chink in armor of segregation. Meanwhile, the Star of Zion and The Christian Reorder of October 5, 1925 are but two of the many newspapers that carried the story and addressed the issue. The former newspaper, an organ of the African Methodist Episcopal Zion Church titled its article 'The Humiliation of a Bishop':

> A special letter from Mrs. C.C. Alleyne, the wife of Bishop Alleyne, resident Bishop of Africa, describes in vivid detail, the humiliation of Bishop W.J. Walls in the restaurant in the Union Station in the capital of the nation, where waves from every mast-pole on the government buildings, the Stars and Stripes over "the land of the free and the brave." In "this land of the free" for which their ancestors suffered and fought, they sat for three hours waiting to be served a meal within sight of the temple of justice, near where laws are made for all the people, and where cars are taken to whisk by the Executive Mansion, all be-lustered with splendor and beauty. It was not until the influence of Bishop Jones, and the local colored press had been invoked that these hungry colored Americans—leaders in the kingdom of God—could be served a meal under the dome of the capital in this "land of the free and home of the brave"—in this happy, holy land of ours that goes into convulsions about liquor, but is sleepy and indifferent about human rights, and

---
102   The African Methodist Episcopal Zion church: Reality of the Black Church. (Charlotte, North Carolina: A.M.E. Zion Publishing House, 1974), p. 519

the treatment accorded colored Americans.

We commend Bishop Walls, and Mrs. Alleyne, the wife of Bishop Alleyne, for the courage they displayed in defying American prejudice in the capital of the Republic where it has increased, rather than diminished under the present administration, from which we can hope for no relief or redress. Mr. Coolidge devotes his energies to keeping cool while the capital seethes with racial discontent, proscription, discrimination beneath his heels. It was never thus under the administration of Grover Cleveland.[103]

"Twelve years later, as far North as Portland, Maine, where he had gone to address the Interracial Fellowship of America, Walls found hotels closed to him until a white judge, Max Pianski, intervened privately on his behalf." (Walls reference #63)[104]

Walls made mention of the Associated Negro Press, at the time headed by Claude Barnett of Chicago and the Rev. L. H. King of the Southwestern Christian Advocate, as supporting the Washington Terminal Dining Room sit-in:

> In refusing to be segregated in the Washington Terminal, Bishop Walls was right, because such segregation is wrong. Nothing sanctions it but its enforcement by a prejudiced majority. To those who cajole themselves on their ability to enforce segregation against the Negro, we must urge that "might is right." Just as the highway man at the point of a gun holds up his helpless victim and strips him of his prized possessions, so the prejudiced preachers of white supremacy, moved by color phobia, armed with the weapon of societal control, hold up the colored American, stripping us of all our

---

103   The Star Of Zion (10/1/25)
104   The Washington Post, October 1, 1925

citizenship rights to free and unhampered concourse in the pursuit and fulfillment of our public duties and responsibilities in the body politic. But those who highhandedly do such things must and will someday discover that there are moral foundations underlying all real prosperity, national and individual, and that any infringement of these laws by the community will result as disastrously as similarly infringement by the individual.

Segregation, (went on the editorial), is the national sequence of nervous paroxysm induced by fears of social contacts on the part of many folk who cannot risk themselves against the probably easy collapse of certain superficial barriers thrown up by belabored effort, between existing social groups, with a view to maintain a certain traditional social theory that has its roots in other days – those days long since, and forever, gone by. By state law, by moral law, and biological law the colored American is entitled to the same equities and freedom of movement, social and political, in American life.[105]

What he began as a young minister, addressing and representing his church at the General Conference of the Methodist Episcopal Church, South, making the Fraternal Address of May 1918 in which he stated "from the ruin of the unhappy sixties that left the Colored man a citizen and freed our civilization both North and South, so that in this country has risen like a phoenix from its ashes," [106] he continued and expanded in the years ahead.

Bishop Walls was not only a long time activist and supporter of the National Association of the Advancement of Colored People, but as he carried

---

105   Ibid, pp. 521-522
106   Walls, Rev. William J. Fraternal Address to the Bishops, Fathers and Brethren of the General Conference of   the Methodist Episcopal Church, South. May 1918, p6.

out his duties as such that in June 13, 1958 he was appealed to as a longtime supporter of the National Association for the Advancement of Colored people.

> Dear Bishop Walls:
>
> As a longtime supporter of the National Association for the Advancement of Colored People, we are certain that you have an understanding of the varied problems currently facing the Association. Many of these problems have been created by those who stand opposed to the full realization of the democratic ideal.
>
> Our leaders in the South have been victimized by economics reprisals, intimidations, violence and a few have lost their lives as a result of participation in the struggle for justice and freedom. Outside the South, as a result of a greatly expanded Negro population in the urban areas and the attention focused upon rising crime, delinquency, disease and housing problems, there has been a studied effort to malign and misinterpret the legitimate aims and aspirations of Negroes by ascribing group guilt and responsibility At a time when the resources of the Association are needed more than ever before to deal with these problems, ...We need your help.
>
> Yours truly,
>
> Channing H. Tobias
> Chairman, Board of Directors

Similarly, letters in the NAACP archives show NAACP Church Secretary, Edward J. Odum, Jr. thanking Bishop Walls. "Thanks again also for the kind assistance you brought to the last NAACP National Convention from your denomination."

IDENTITY OF THE CHURCH

A major part of Bishop Wall's contribution to the Church was his description of the identity of African Methodist Episcopal Zion Church. In a major article published in 1954, called 'The Place of the Negro Church in History', Bishop Walls sets out his view of the nature and identity of African Methodist Episcopal Zion Church.

He starts the article musing on the question of whether the emergence of Black churches was enforced (by White denominations making it difficult for African Americans to belong) or voluntary. He concludes that it was voluntary and therefore "the Negro Church was the first movement in his [i.e. the Black man] own flight for freedom."[107] He develops this insight using five distinctive themes.

Bishop Walls begins by drawing attention to the remarkable list of leaders in the campaign against slavery and for civil rights that came from the African Methodist Episcopal Zion Church. He explains: "It is significant that the major leaders in the fight for freedom, with few exceptions, have come from the independent Negro Church. Notably, a few were: Joseph C. Price, Bishop James Walker Hood, and Bishop Alexander Walters of the A. M. E. Zion Church."[108] Later in the article he lists Harriet Tubman (her significance will be discussed further in the next section of this chapter) and the advisor to President Abraham Lincoln, Frederick Douglass. Bishop Walls is making the important point that this distinctive denomination created a space for the Black person to be truly free.

---

107 Bishop William Walls, 'The Place of the Negro Church in History' in Bishop William Walls, <u>Connectionalism and the Negro Church.</u> (private papers,1954) pp. 11.
108 Ibid.

Bishop Walls' second theme is the importance of the connection with Methodism--the African Methodist Episcopal Zion Church is legitimized by its connected with a major branch of Christendom. This is not a sect outside the official branches of the Christian family. "Connectionalism" – as Bishop Walls calls it – is a vital part of the Church's identity. It is the connection not simply with Methodism, but with the Christian tradition and the expectations in terms of appropriate behavior which is part of that tradition.

Walls next addresses "self-government." African Americans had not been given the opportunity to run anything until the formation of the Black church. Bishop Walls writes:

> It proved to be the first school of self-government for our race group in America. After the separation of the Negro connections from the General Methodist Church ... the serious work of self-government began. Its main objective has been freedom: freedom of choice in religion, freedom from race domination by the slaveholding race, and freedom to worship God under our vine and fig tree.[109]

Given this experience, it is not surprising that the independent Black churches produced some of the finest leadership of the African American community.

The fourth theme is modeling leadership for the young in the African American community. Again, in a society where racism is widespread, there is a lack of appropriate role models for young African Americans. African American leaders, most especially those in the Church, can be leadership role models for young African Americans. Bishop Walls speaks very movingly of the practice of honoring the leadership in the Church. He writes: "one of the significant things that was always done when the older ones of us were children,

---

[109] Ibid.

and which impressed us with deep reverence for our church and leadership, causing sweet reflection on memory and history, was the practice of draping the middle pulpit chair with mourning cloth when a bishop died anywhere in Zion."[110] One point that Bishop Walls makes central is that it is important that a respect and affection for leadership is cultivated in the young (Appendix One). For the Bishop, this is not simply a modeling for young people, but the cultivation of an appropriate attitude to leadership.

The fifth and final theme is a summary of the first four themes and an invitation to dive further into the initial vision of the African Methodist Episcopal Zion Church. It is a call for renewal and for a family spirit to shape the tradition. It is a recommendation that the Bishops are more involved in visiting their congregations. It is a call for the Church to be "alert as never before to foreign missions and home missions."[111]

HARRIET TUBMAN HOME

Bishop Walls played many a role in the life of the African Methodist Episcopal Zion Church, including facilitating the maintenance of a gift only now coming into its own: the national treasury bequeathed to it by one of her daughters, the Harriet Tubman Home.

Harriet Ross Tubman is one of, if not the, most well known conductors of the Underground Railroad. Born into slavery in Dorchester County, Maryland, she was raised under the harshest of conditions. At twelve she was seriously injured by a blow to the head, inflicted by her white overseer, for not helping to stop a male slave from escaping. Harriet married John Tubman, a

---
110   Ibid.
111   Ibid.

free African American at age twenty-five. Five years later she feared she would be sold so she escaped. She was given a piece of paper by a White neighbor with two names and told how to find the first house on her railroad to freedom. This was her introduction to the Underground Railroad. In 1851 she relocated her family to St. Catherine's Ontario, Canada. Harriet later returned to Maryland and led, it is believed, over 300 persons from the South to freedom through the Underground Railroad. During her life she also worked as a scout and soldier in the Civil War with the Union Army, and as a nurse and performing other notable deeds for which she was received and honored at the White House by President Lincoln.

In June 1896, Harriet Tubman bought, to the astonishment of her neighbors, (she was one of very few Blacks in the area) a farm, which she had looked at and yearned for daily, in Auburn, New York. She paid $1,250 for this farm which she wanted to establish as a home for the aged, especially ministers. It is said that at one time the great Harriet thought of calling her dream the John Brown Home and in 1903, she deeded 25 acres and her home to the African Methodist Episcopal Zion Church.

The Harriet Tubman property, willed to The African Methodist Episcopal Zion Church by Tubman, consists of two major houses, a barn and some smaller buildings on the premises. One of the two houses was her own residence. The other was a two-story frame which was constructed for aged men and women. It was operated successfully with people taken care of on an institutional plan. In the spring of 1913 Harriet became ill and was admitted to "The Home," and remained there until her death later that year. Her funeral was held in the

Thompson AME Zion Church in Auburn where she was a devout member. She was buried in Fort Hill Cemetery, approximately 100 yards from the church.

In 1944 the City ordered the house to be wrecked unless restorations of the buildings were immediately undertaken. Bishop William Jacob Walls, then in charge of the Western New York Conference asked for time to have them re-erected and city authorities granted his request. Under the leadership of Bishop Walls, the Home was restored and a garage added. The Home was dedicated in 1953. Authorized by the Connectional Council of 1945, Dr. H. B. Shaw and the Bishop of the Western New York Conference went forward to reconstruct the residence, and the old one destroyed and carried away.

Bishop William J. Walls made a strong appeal for the involvement of young people in the life of the Harriet Tubman Home. Said he: "Since school children built the monument to Daniel De Foe who wrote Robinson Crusoe, over his grave in London, it would be a thing of honor and joy for the colored youth and the children of Zion to build with their nickels and dimes a Harriet Tubman Institution as a shrine for American youth and inspiration to take courage there from and move on to the better things in the upward way." While there are Tubman homes and monuments all over the country, those who built them do not have her property to build on.

Sixty-six years after Bishop Walls' intervention to save the property Bishop George W.C. Walker, Sr. has moved the program of this Home to a higher level. (See Appendix Two). Many trumpets are being sounded and fanfare is made, but Bishop Walls' role in maintaining the property will never be forgotten. All that takes place in this twenty-first century certainly compliments and leads to the fulfillment of Bishop Walls' vision, for in his report at the 36th Quadrennial session of the African Methodist Episcopal Zion Church held in Buffalo, New York, May 4-18, 1960, he, as Presiding Prelate of the First Episcopal District which included the Western New York Conference, in his address said:

> the dream of Harriet Tubman was an Old People's Home and a Home for the Orphans, and I do not doubt that it will be realized someday when the A.M.E. Zion Church will become able and alert to accomplish it. No such grand old historic person, whose name is memorialized in the battle of freedom all over the country and the world, should be forever neglected by her church to which she gave freely her earthly heritage, and which shares her immortal name.[112]

DOROTHY WALLS CAMP

As he moved about preaching, providing pastoral oversight and expanding the borders of Zion Methodism, Bishop Walls acted in a supervisory capacity as Bishop but was aware of the awesome responsibility of the of spiritual development of the souls in his care. Holding the reigns of educational responsibility yet giving guidance and preparation to individuals who had to live in a world that kept them from so much, Bishop Walls sought ways to meet basic needs of the people he served. One such need was the provision of a suitable camp site for their use since people of color could not share facilities

---

112   Bishop William J. Walls. <u>Report of the First Episcopal District, African Methodist Episcopal Zion Church</u> at the Thirty-Sixth Quadrennial Session of the African Methodist Episcopal Zion Church (Buffalo, New York: May-4-18, 1960), p.6

owned by White churches or private entities and any one or small group of Black churches was usually too poor to own any such site. It was a need that never was far away from his consciousness. He may not always have remembered, but he never forgot.

His work in the Western New York Conference and the Harriet Tubman Home underscored the need for useable, larger, similar facilities elsewhere. In the summer of 1934, what then became known as Camp Barber (not currently functioning), a "310 acre property with two lakes, owned by the A.M.E. Zion Church in the Berkshire Mountains"[113] was also set aside for recreational purposes and as a camp ground since the church "was slow in developing the Barber Memorial Home there."[114]

The Bishop did not forget those in the South. He never forgot how, in spite of all he had to face growing up, the quiet and peace of the mountains had ministered to his soul. And this idea which kept percolating through his subconscious as it were, finally filtered upward, and 33 years after ascending the episcopacy, in 1957, Bishop William J. Walls, then presiding Prelate of the Western North Carolina Conference, appointed an investigative committee with the sole intention of purchasing a camp site.

Alive in his memory were the breathtaking, scenic views of the towering blue mountains, at Chimney Rock; the place where the beauty of nature was enough to bring one closer to the love of the creator of the universe. Hence, when a tuberculosis infirmary located in that area closed its doors and it was

---

113   Bishop William J. Walls. <u>The African Methodist Episcopal Zion church: Reality of the Black Church.</u> (Charlotte, North Carolina: A.M.E. Zion Publishing House, 1974), p. 519
114   <u>Ibid.</u>

learned that the Royal League of Illinois was selling this property, Bishop Walls was not slow either in appointing or encouraging a conference committee to actively do further investigation of the suggested site.

So it was that the conference purchased 66 acres in the foothills of Black Mountain, North Carolina in the Blue Ridge Mountains, with one significant major building and other small buildings and encompassed the area of major religious assemblies.

In his report to the thirty-sixth quadrennial session of the African Methodist Episcopal Zion Church held in Buffalo, New York, May 4-18, 1960, Bishop Walls, then Presiding Prelate of the First Episcopal District which included Western North Carolina said:

> We have purchased a camp at Black Mountain, North Carolina two years ago, as the possession of the Western North Carolina Conference, which contains sixty-one acres of land, facility for a lake when conditions of the contract are lived out, has a magnificent building one time used as a rest sanitarium, capable of accommodating fifty persons, with a large lobby and upper and lower porches half way around it, and beautifully trimmed and modernized with city facilities in a country district. It is our plan to put another building on the camp, which we are now working out. This is definitely one of the greatest achievements and progressive steps forward of any one annual conference of our Zion in this new day as they provide for our young and old alike, spiritual and physical education, with wholesome recreation and worship, in this beautiful mountain area, surrounded by major Protestant Assembly Grounds.[115]

---

115   Bishop William J. Walls. <u>Report of the First Episcopal District, African Methodist Episcopal Zion Church</u> at the Thirty-Sixth Quadrennial Session of the African Methodist Episcopal Zion Church (Buffalo, New York: May-4-18, 1960), p.8

TELLING A NEGLECTED STORY

In 1965, a project undertaken by the Youth of the First Episcopal District of the African Methodist Episcopal Zion Church was the production of a publication entitled, "Reverence of a Senior Bishop" in tribute to Bishop William Jacob Walls on his 80th birthday (and his 41st anniversary as a Bishop). A portion of the foreword gives insight into how the youth of this denomination regarded this Bishop and his unswerving efforts on their behalf:

> We therefore pledge to join hands, North and South, unite our forces, and walk with our peerless leader to help him accomplish the work closest to his heart: namely, the development and perpetuation of our A.M.E. Zion Summer Camp for youth, the Harriet Tubman Home, our secondary schools, recruitment of young ministers, and other enterprises for the enhancement and continued growth of our church, at home and abroad, for world redemption. To Bishop Walls - we pledge our loyalty and devotion to the causes of Christ.[116]

George Wallace Maze, III said it best:

> Several years ago many people were in doubt when Bishop William Jacob Walls stirred the thinking caps of the Western North Carolina conference about purchasing a Camp in the beautiful mountains of Black Mountain, North Carolina. There were all types of statements negative and positive, whether they should purchase the camp or not. Then there came along the hope that was needed when the people and ministers and many other friends thought that this would be an ideal place for the Negro boy and girl of North Carolina and elsewhere to come and enjoy the beautiful nature of God

---

[116] Revs. H.D. Bonner, L.L. Smith et al. <u>Reverence of a Senior Bishop</u> (First Episcopal District: First Church 1965)p.12

in the heart of the mountains. Off the streets and out of the slums, they will go to Camp Dorothy Walls. They will learn there, through Christian teaching that God has willed the children of the sun to come forth from the dusty plains of Egypt to surmount the wings of progress in the mountains of Camp Dorothy Walls.[117]

Said one writer: "under the leadership of Bishop George Walker, Sr., and Mrs. Geraldine Walker, and the work and dedication of the members of the Piedmont Episcopal District, the facility has gone from a camp to a retreat center — from great to Grand."[118] The camp, purchased by the Western North Carolina Conference in 1958, was officially opened in September the same year and dedicated as Camp Dorothy Walls in honor of the wife of Bishop Walls. Since that time, state of the art buildings have been erected, and the campus has undergone considerable renovation and upgrading.[119] Some of the visionary bishops who have followed in the footsteps of Bishop William Jacob Walls and have sustained the work he started as it pertains to Camp Dorothy Walls have been: Bishop Raymond Luther Jones, Bishop William Milton Smith, Bishop Ruben Lee Speaks, Bishop Cecil Bishop, and Bishop George W.C. Walker, Sr. Throughout its 52 years of existence thus far, the camp has undoubtedly lived up to what Bishop Wall's vision and been a place where individuals retreat, fellowship and restoration.

RELIGIOUS EDUCATION

From childhood, Bishop William Jacob Walls led a busy life. He juggled jobs,

---

[117] Ibid. p.67
[118] Mattie W. Taylor. Writer Editor "Camp Dorothy Walls" in THE GOOD NEWS (Brooklyn, New York: First A.M.E Zion Church: January 2010)
[119] Mattie W. Taylor. Writer Editor "Camp Dorothy Walls" in THE GOOD NEWS (Brooklyn, New York: First A.M.E Zion Church: January 2010)

grade school, and church school, play time and house chores. As eldest of his siblings, he was ever cognizant of his mother's efforts, and her emphasis on his achievement of excellence in studies and religious growth and development. Time supports the theory that, throughout his life, he treasured her teachings as he did her, having kept her by his side as he grew and served in various capacities in the church until her passing in May 16, 1956.

As a young man in Zion, Walls is said to have attended a meeting in Toronto with James W. Eichelberger, Jr. who would later become the first International General Secretary Treasurer, of Christian Education. Their relationship remained fruitful and amicable for many years:

> Eichelberger and Rev. Walls began to work incessantly for an improved religious education program (for the denomination). Mr. Eichelberger wrote articles and editorialized in the paper then operated by the Sunday School Department, The Sunday School Headlight. Reverend Walls wrote a series of articles to The Star of Zion in the interest of this cause and circulated a pamphlet entitled What Youth Wants[120].

Several oral resources, including Hoggard, credit Walls with prolific work throughout his tenure. For example, "from 1941-1964, pastoral appointments in the New York Conference increased from thirty-nine to seventy-four, and four new churches were established in Bronx alone."[121]

Throughout his busy tenure as Bishop, Walls maintained a keen interest in sharing the Gospel and spreading Zion Methodism in Africa. Although other bishops like Hebert Bell Shaw and Reuben Lee Speaks were more instrumental

---

120　　Bishop William J. Walls. The African Methodist Episcopal Zion Church: Reality of the Black Church Charlotte, (North Carolina: A.M.E. Zion Publishing House, 1974)p, 291.
121　　Ibid.

in implementing Africa outreach programs, the Dorothy J. Walls School in Po River, Liberia is not the only place overseas that felt Bishop Wall's touch. Indeed, he is credited with leading the First Episcopal District in 1954 to establish what was then called an "African Memorial Bank to raise money for work in Africa,"[122] the Cartwright Memorial A.M.E. Zion Church in Brewerville, Liberia being the first to benefit by way of its restoration. While he had few hands-on roles in the actualization of the A.M.E. Zion Churches, churches have been named after him to honor him as an early visionary of what is now a vibrant and expansive A.M.E. Zion witness in mission outreach. In 2010, there were more than two dozen churches bearing the name of Bishop Walls in the Western West Africa Conferences alone. In Yonkers, New York one street is named for him - Bishop William Jacob Walls Place. In 1960 prior to the independence of many African nations Walls stated: "Bishop Walls is remembered by laity and clergy alike as a lover of the church who worked arduously for the upbuilding of God and Zion." Said one minister, "Bishop Walls was a dictator for the good of the church. Everything he had he left to the church."[123] But more than that, it is felt by many who knew him, that he set the agenda for the denomination and helped re-write the Book of Discipline.

Having served for 44 years, Bishop William Jacob Walls made his final Episcopal Report at the 38th Quadrennial Session of the General Conference of the African Methodist Episcopal Zion Church which met in Detroit, Michigan, May 1-15, 1968. It is worthy to note that this freedom fighter dedicated his report to Reverend Dr. Martin Luther King, Jr., noting that it was done

> In memory of this man who gave his precious life for equality,

---

122 Ibid.
123 Harrison D. Bonner. Interview. January 1`0, 2007, Waterbury, CT.

human welfare, and dignity of all, in the spirit of peace and non-violence, while we, as Christians, acknowledge to be the Christ-like way. Let the soul chords of freedom in Martin Luther King, Jr. vibrate in us now and through us to mankind in all ages. To love Jesus, God's Son, is to love and work for the freedom of mankind.[124]

Dr. King recognized Bishop Walls' years of service in a letter included in this report entitled, one of our significant letters from Dr. King (See Appendix Three). Bishop William Jacob Walls was a venerable preacher, a respected preacher amongst his peers (See Appendix Four).

A protégé of Bishop James Walker Hood, he, like most Bishops of the African Methodist Episcopal Zion church, knew how to carry a firm hand in a velvet glove. When it came to applying the law of the church he did not abide any mediocre performance, he tolerated no slackness at any level of leadership at the local church level when it came to applying the law of the church. He details this clearly in recounting the problems and their resolution as pertained to the Metropolitan A.M.E. Zion Church at Hartford, CT as it was being relocated from Pearl Street to its present edifice on Main Street in 1926, led by its then pastor, Rev. A.J. Gorham.

> The transition, at first, did not turn out well. All the trustees that engineered the move were white, with the exception of one Negro on the board. In the course of a very few years, the money entrusted to the trustees from the sale of Pear Street, for the most part, disappeared. The Main Street property deal included two houses across the street from the church, one used for the parsonage and the other rented. Gross

---

124   Bishop William J. Walls. <u>Report of the First Episcopal District</u> at the 38th Quadrennial Session, African Methodist Episcopal Zion Church,(Detroit, Michigan, 1968) p.5

85

irregularities were discovered in the management by these trustees; the cash money left in their hands was discovered to be badly used, unaccounted for, and unverified. Pastor Gorham discovered this and he was directed by the bishop (Walls) to put the matter in civil court. The result was the discharge of the trustees and the ruling of the court that only members of the church could be trustees. This episode caused much hardship and grief to Rev. Gorham. It began a new day for this church, which has prospered ever since.[125]

---

125 Bishop William J. Walls. The African Methodist Episcopal Zion Church: Reality of the Black Church Charlotte, (North Carolina: A.M.E. Zion Publishing House, 1974)p, 259.

CHAPTER FIVE

BISHOP STEPHEN GILL SPOTTSWOOD: THE IMPACT OF HIS LIFE, LEADERSHIP AND LEGACY ON THE AFRICAN METHODIST EPISCOPAL ZION CHURCH

Stephen Gill Spottswood was born on July 18, 1897 in Boston, Massachusetts, the only child of Abram Lincoln and Mary Elizabeth Gray Spottswood. Though history is silent on the first twenty years of his life, he must have been gainfully employed studying, for he earned "a B.A. degree in 1917 from Albright College, Reading, Pa., and a Th.B degree from Gordon Divinity School in Boston in 1919 and did graduate study at Yale University in 1923 and 1924. Fifteen years later, in 1939, Livingstone College awarded him an honorary D.D."[126]

One source, Spottswood AME Zion Church,[127] states that in 1909 his family moved to Freeport, Maine. While details or ramifications of his growth and development are not generally available, one oral source speaks to the ever-burning zeal for equality and first-class citizenship which developed in his heart while yet a child:

---

126   Bishop James Clinton Hoggard,. The African Methodist Episcopal Zion Church, 1972-1996: A Bicentennial Commemorative History. (Charlotte, North Carolina: A.M.E. Zion Publishing House, 1998), p. 460.
127   Rev. Dr. Adebola T. Odukoya. Spottswood AME Zion Church: 58 Years of Faithful Testimony(Denver, Co., Spottswood AME Zion Church, 29005), p. 14

raised in a restrictive New England town, when a child, discovered from his playmates that he was different. This molded his attitude to be equal. Closely akin to his interest in his church, was his zeal for the welfare of his race. He worked ardently in local and state chapters of the NAACP in every city and town which he had pastored."[128]

Stephen Gil Spottswood entered the traveling ministry through the New England Conference. This much is very clear, but questions still arise as to the date he began to preach; one identifiable source corroborating this account of his early years is Spottswood's obituary by the Nation Association of Advancement of Colored People, in its official publication, The Crisis, which stated that "even before he was ordained as an AME Zion minister in 1920, he served for two years as pastor in West Newton and Lowell, Mass,"[129] suggesting that he would have had to have been admitted into the traveling ministry in early 1918. The official documents were not available to the writer (and questions exist about their existence in any archives and or availability), but based on the information of all three of the official historians of the denomination, Bradley,[130] Hoggard[131] and Walls, we understand that "he entered the traveling ministry through the New England Conference, in 1919, and was appointed to West Newton and Lowell, Mass." Being admitted to the traveling ministry did not mean being ordained, but it certainly means that he was admitted at least eleven months,

---

128   William J. Walls, The African Methodist Episcopal Zion Church: Reality of the Black Church (Charlotte, North Carolina: A.M.E. Zion Publishing House, 1974), p. 530
129   . Crisis Editorials: "Bishop Stephen Gill Spottswood" in The Crisis. Official Organ of the National Association for the Advancement of Colored People (New York, New York: Crisis Publishing Corporation, February 1975), p. 41.
130   David Henry Bradley, Sr. A History of the A.M.E. ZION CHURH: Part II 1872-1968: (Nashville: Tennessee, The Parthenon Press, 1970), p. 441.
131   Bishop J. Clinton Hoggard. The African Methodist Episcopal Zion Church, 1872-1996: A Bicentennial Commemorative History (Charlotte, North Carolina: A.M.E. Zion Publishing House, 1998), p 460.

closer to one year, and prior to his ordination."[132] Bishop Hoggard[133] confirms the same, noting that the first ordination took place on Thursday, February 5, 1920 and the second about four months later on Sunday, June 20, 1920. Further argument still holds for the possibility of unforeseen circumstances leading to one holding such a position before being admitted to the traveling ministry. Yet again we can thank Bishop Hoggard for corroboration as he notes that he (Spottswood) "was a pastor for thirty-four years."[134] As will be addressed later, he was elevated to the episcopacy in 1952. This discrepancy only serves to underscore the need for well-maintained archives.

The year 1919 must have been very memorable to Stephen Gill Spottswood. He graduated from Divinity School, he entered the traveling ministry and the annals of history tells us that on Tuesday, June 10, 1919 he took to himself a wife, Viola Estelle Booker, a marriage which lasted until her death on October 24, 1953.

The newly ordained Spottswood's pastoral work to God and Zion began by serving in West Newton and Lowell, MA and afterward served as pastor, Green Memorial Church, Portland Maine. Others appointments included: Varick, New Haven, CT, Goler Memorial, Winston -Salem: Jones Tabernacle, Indianapolis, IN; St. Juke, Buffalo, NY; and John Wesley Church, Washington, D.C. It was while he served as pastor of John Wesley that he is not only credited with increasing the membership from 600 to 3,000, but the

---

132   William J. Walls, The African Methodist Episcopal Zion Church: Reality of the Black Church (Charlotte, North Carolina: A.M.E. Zion Publishing House, 1974), p. 609
133   Bishop James Clinton Hoggard,. The African Methodist Episcopal Zion Church, 1972-1996: A Bicentennial Commemorative History. (Charlotte, North Carolina: A.M.E. Zion Publishing House, 1998), p. 460.
134   Ibid.

following was written of him:

> The coming of the Reverend Stephen Gill Spottswood in 1936 began what is known as the era of "an expanded ministry." His "Temple Beautiful Campaign" resulted in major renovations and redecoration. The Reverend Spottswood's labors were successfully directed toward the association, recreation, stewardship, and social service." All church debts were eliminated. The Reverend Spottswood gave the worship service a greater liturgical character with the use of chants, canticles and acolyte guild.
>
> At the Thirty-First Session of the General Conference of the A.M.E. Zion Church held at John Wesley in 1940, a resolution was passed which officially designated John Wesley as the National Church of Zion Methodism.[135]

In 1919, Spottswood began what became a parallel lifetime career lasting as long as his pastoral calling and which spoke to the needs of individuals just as much, becoming a member of the National Association for the Advancement of Colored People (NAACP), the organization to which he would not only hold membership, but to which he would rise to the position of President of the Washington D.C. branch. The earliest of our historical writers, Dr. Bradley said: "Stephen Gill Spottswood has been closely identified with the National Association for the Advancement of Colored People, serving for several years as the Chairman of the Board. A brilliant legal mind, he also served as the head of the denominational Board of Finance (Chairman) and as a trustee of Livingstone College."[136] In his years of service, Spottswood was, in turn, the

---

[135] James David Armstrong. <u>A Review of a History of John Wesley A.M.E. Zion Church, Washington D.C.</u>
[136] David Henry Bradley, Sr. <u>A History of the A.M.E. ZION CHURH: Part II 1872-1968:</u> (Nashville: Tennessee, The Parthenon Press, 1970), pp. 441-442

TELLING A NEGLECTED STORY

Presiding Prelate of the South Mississippi, West Tennessee and Mississippi, Oklahoma, Texas, and North Arkansas Conferences; the Ohio, Michigan, Allegheny, and Indiana Conferences; the Colorado, New England, Virgin Islands, and South American Conferences; and Philadelphia-Baltimore and Central North Carolina Conferences. A quarter of a century after his passing he is still vividly remembered. Churches have been erected with his assistance, urging and encouragement. "Spottswood AME Zion Church: 53 Years of Faith Testimony" includes a tribute to its namesake:

> Many Churches of the AME Zion denomination named after him spread from USA to Africa. We at Denver really appreciated the opportunity to share in his life and works and the ministry that he was a contributive part. The Denver Church, organized by a few faithful Zionites, came about through a petition to Bishop Spottswood to establish a Church in Denver, Colorado. The Bishop approved the petition and the church came into existence on December 2, 1952. Being elected a Bishop in 1952, the Rt. Rev. Stephen Gill Spottswood became the first African Methodist Episcopal Zion leader in the Rocky-Mountain region.[137]

Bradley obviously knew of the deep bonds that existed there for in his history book one reads: "one of the youngest conferences of the denomination, the Colorado, was organized by Bishop Stephen Gill Spottswood (organized December 7, 1952) and reported to the General Conference of 1956."[138] Bishop Spottswood was also very involved in overseas work and is credited with initiating mission banquets in the state side conferences specifically to raise

---

137   Rev. Dr. Adebola T. Odukoya. <u>Spottswood AME Zion Church: 53 Years of Faithful Testimony</u>. (Denver, Co.: Spottswood AME Zion Church, 2005), p. 10.
138   David Henry Bradley, Sr. <u>A History of The A.M.E. Zion Church: Part II 1872-1968</u>. (Nashville, Tennessee: The Parthenon Press, 1970) pp. 63-64

funds to assist the work in these overseas mission conferences. Among the areas known to benefit from these were the Virgin Island Conference, the Guyana Conference, along with those in Barbados and the South African Republic. He presided over these conferences. Many churches are named in his honor and memory, not only across the areas where he served, but indeed throughout Zion.

Despite myriad episcopal commitments, Bishop Spottswood was never too busy to think of the physical needs of the youth of his district and provide sources of recreation, no doubt to keep them gainfully employed and out of trouble. He, like other bishops of his day, endeavored to advance the cause of summer retreats. Thus Walls tells us that "in 1961 the Ohio Conference purchased a 30 acre park from the Ohio Council of Churches for camping purposes, and dedicated it to the memory of Viola Booker Spottswood, late wife and missionary supervisor of the presiding bishop of Ohio, Stephen Gill Spottswood. The camp opened officially during the summer of 1963."[139]

Bishop Spottswood is often spoken of with regard to his years of service as a member of the Methodist Council, the National Council of Churches and the General Commission on Chaplains and Armed Service Personnel. However, much of this interest and work, like his work with the N.A.A.C.P., did not start when he ascended to the episcopacy. The 2009 Great Gathering of the three major Black Methodist bodies in the USA, the African Methodist Episcopal Church, the Christian Methodist Episcopal Church and the African Methodist Episcopal Zion Church called to mind that fact that since 1868

---

[139] William J. Walls, The African Methodist Episcopal Zion Church: Reality of the Black Church (Charlotte, North Carolina: A.M.E. Zion Publishing House, 1974), p. 349

there hadn't been a call to Organic Union. The Reverend Dr. Stephen Gill Spottswood at the Fourth Annual Pastor's and Christian workers' Conference, Lincoln University, Pa., July 13, 1939, is quoted as saying: "It seems that the spiritual implications of Organic Union--the mere categorical visioning of the spiritual forces which would be released through the merger of Negro Methodists--should give us sufficient impulse to proceed deliberately toward this high goal of unity."[140] Spottswood went further to make clear the stance of his denomination, stressing the fact that it had not changed in spite of the sum total of actions by members of the Union. Firstly, he addressed the fact that in spite of good will gestures, where the bishops of the A.M.E. Zion Church acted in good faith, several maneuvers eventually led to the resolution tabled on the matter in 1872. Says Walls:

> This action, which had taken place on Tuesday, May 19, prompted a sinewy editorial in the official organ of the A.M.E. Zion Church The Zion's Standard and Weekly Review, on May 20, 1868, an extract of which stated: "The A.M.E. Zion Connection, having carefully kept within the bounds of the Platform as agreed upon by the two Connections, comes forward to make good her agreement as agreed and say--"we are ready," ready to unite upon one common platform. We are ready to make common cause with you for the up building of the Church of Christ. We are ready to meet the demands of the People; for the good of the People, we are ready to sacrifice all our own interests, views, differences and mode of electing Executives that the cause of Christ and His People shall be advanced here on earth. We are ready to meet with you and to sacrifice our connection name that we may present to the

---

140 I David Henry Bradley, Sr. A History of The A.M.E. Zion Church: Part II 1872-1968. (Nashville, Tennessee: The Parthenon Press, 1970) p. 353

world a UNITED AFRICAN METHODIST CHURCH IN AMERICA, and the response is for THE ADOPTION OF A NEW PLATFORM. To this we demure. We now leave the matter, and let it never be said, that Zion was the cause of the future division between the A.M.E and the A.M.E Zion Connections, for WE WERE READY.[141]

Spottswood further illustrated the attitude of his denomination on Organic Union, calling to memory the facts of sub-committees appointed by bishops of the African Methodist Episcopal and the A.M.E Zion Churches deliberated and seven articles of agreement were reached. These were remanded to the annual and quarterly conference of the two denominations. Subsequently at the bequest of the Bishops they were distributed for use in the voting process at the local level Organic Union. But Zion's leadership did not have to wait for the results of the vote to show where it stood. As Spottswood said:

> "To illustrate the attitude of the African Methodist Episcopal Zion Church on organic union, let us cite for example the case of churches in Wilkes-Barre, Pennsylvania, and Elmira, New York. In both of these cities Zion and Bethel had churches. The Negro Methodist Churches operating in the same city, so the bishops of each denomination met and agreed, because of the discussion of organic union was then extant, to the following compromise. The Zion Church was to abandon the field in Wilkes-Barre where the Bethel Church was the stronger and the Bethel Church was to abandon the field in Elmira where the Zion Church was the stronger. Zion promptly withdrew at Wilkes-Barre but Bethel has not withdrawn from Elmira unto this day (July 12, 1939). Zion still retains the ascendency in Elmira but the work of Kingdom is retarded by

---

[141] William J. Walls, The African Methodist Episcopal Zion Church: Reality of the Black Church (Charlotte, North Carolina: A.M.E. Zion Publishing House, 1974), p. 464

the unnecessary competition. We have never attempted any retaliatory tactics in Wilkes-Barre."[142]

Thus did he continue, citing example after example showing how the African Methodist Episcopal Zion Church has always stood ready to unite. 2004-2012 Senior Bishop of the A.M.E. Zion Church, the Right Reverend George Washington Carver Walker, Sr. addressed this:

> When over 6,000 people from African Methodist denominations from across America came together last month for the Great Gathering, most people would assume they were having a revival. And in essence, that is exactly what happened in Columbia, S.C. But indeed, there was so much more. We were called together by God. Members of the African Methodist Episcopal (AME) Church, African Methodist Zion (AMEZ) Church, and the Christian Methodist Episcopal (CME) Church united over three days to formulate a plan to help stem the tide of unemployment, incarceration, high dropout rates, and other problems that are destroying young African American males. The numbers are absolutely chilling. There are more 17-year-old-black males in prison than in college. One in four black males, age 20-24, are high school dropouts. According to the Center for Disease Control, homicide is the leading cause of death among African American males 15 to 34 years of age. African American males have seven times the AIDS rate of non-Hispanic white males and are 1.5 times more likely to have high blood pressure. University scholars and researchers could talk and debate for years about the reasons for these sobering statistics. Preachers can stand in pulpits on Sunday morning and deliver eloquent sermons to their congregations about the problems. Almost

---
142   David Henry Bradley, Sr. <u>A History of The A.M.E. Zion Church: Part II 1872-1968</u>. (Nashville, Tennessee: The Parthenon Press, 1970) p. 354

all African Americans know of someone - a brother, cousin, nephew, uncle, father, friend, or neighbor that fits the profile. Although we will always have people discussing these issues and publishing reports, this is a major crisis that the black church must confront head on, the same way the church dealt with Civil Rights and race relations in the 1960s. So after three days of meetings, discussions and worshiping God, we left Columbia with a plan. Our Great Gathering devised a Male Investment Plan designed to combat some of the ills facing African American Males, the African American Community, and the larger social fabric here in the United States. We call it a Male Investment Plan because we believe we have to put our time, talents, and financial resources into teaching, coaching, and shaping the lives of young black males to bring about a change in their attitude about life and living. They have to learn how to respect themselves first before they can learn how to respect others. The key component of the Male Investment Plan is based upon Saturday Academies that will be held at AME, AMEZ and CME churches across the nation. Some of the goals of the Academies include improving education, spiritual training and growth, conflict resolution, health, career counseling, and financial literacy. The Academies are the beginning and will serve as the cornerstone of our plan to help correct the serious problems plaguing our young African American males. Our plan also requires the churches to work very closely with historically black colleges and universities and other institutions of higher learning in their area. We know we do not have all the answers but we have to start somewhere and we have to start now. We have waited too long to address these problems and now we're facing a major crisis. One of the responsibilities of the church is to address societal ills and through faith in God, strive to correct the situations. It has always been one of the foundations of the African

Methodist denominations. A great example is Haiti. Even before the earthquake ravaged the small country, the AME and CME churches were already in that country working in missions, schools, and clinics to help those in need. It is what God requires the church to do. We must help those in need and individuals who are down trodden. As I stated earlier, we cannot rectify the myriad of problems facing young African American males by ourselves. But the African Methodist Male Investment Plan is a start. If you are concerned about the future of America's young people, join us as we mount a movement to rescue the next generation of young black males. Collectively, we have 5 million members in our denominations and we're committed to raising $10 million from our congregations. But we're going to need support from the private sector, foundations, nonprofit organizations and other faith-based entities to provide human capital, time, and financial resources. This is truly a major movement to make America a better place for our children and our children's children.

It is impossible to separate the work of this servant of God from that done in his church and that as a member of the NAACP. It was good and somewhat expected of those within the church to say it, but refreshing and befitting when others beyond the walls utter those words of positive reception, appreciation and gratitude for the toil and care Bishop Spottswood dedicated his life to doing. Such an outpouring of support came at his death: "On the church, Bishop Spottswood was respected as a dynamic cleric, as well as an aggressive civil rights worker. He was a staunch believer in the Constitution of the United States and an exemplar of the principles of the Christian Church."[143]

---

143   Crisis Editorials: "Bishop Stephen Gill Spottswood" in The Crisis. Official Organ of the National Association for the Advancement of Colored People (New York, New York: Crisis Publishing Corporation, February 1975), p. 41.

Further,

> he was the kind of minister who believed in freedom of the soul on this side of the Jordan as well as during eternity. He was no 'pie-in-the-sky' preacher, and didn't' spend his time with messages about golden slippers and milk and honey in Heaven. He had an insatiable thirst for freedom for the soul here and now. If ever there was a black leader with a unique combination of the will to serve his God and his fellow man that person was Bishop Stephen Gill Spottswood. He set an excellent example for his colleagues in serving well his church and fellow men.[144]

Indeed, his fight for equality was not limited to his work as a member of either group: "He was courageous both as a pastor and a bishop. While serving as bishop in the Deep South, he encountered opposition in Mississippi and Arkansas, and had some dangerous experiences."[145] Further, Spottswood has been described as "more liberal in what he allowed his preachers and laymen to do. He would give young men appointments, unlike some of his fellow Bishops at the time."[146]

Spottswood in his role as a civil rights activist was no different from the man serving at John Wesley Church, Washington, D.C. As he did in his other congregations, his second career impacted his work at his local church:

> The Reverend Spottswood's productive leadership of John

---

[144] "Stephen Gill Spottswood" in <u>The Crisis</u>. Official Organ of the National Association for the Advancement of Colored People (New York, New York: Crisis Publishing Corporation, February 1975), p. 49.
[145] David Henry Bradley, Sr. <u>A History of The A.M.E. Zion Church: Part II 1872-1968</u>. (Nashville, Tennessee: The Parthenon Press, 1970) p. 354
[146] Interview. Dr. Harrison Bonner. January 10, 2007

TELLING A NEGLECTED STORY

Wesley Church was accompanied by conspicuous and extensive work and the affairs of the A.M.E. Zion Denomination and the Washington community. His much lauded leadership of John Wesley Church continued to 1952, when it was honored by his election to the office of Bishop in the A.M..E. Zion Church. His service as pastor, rendered for sixteen years, exceeded that of any of his predecessors.[147]

So Spottswood served his church and served the organization of the NAACP continuously, albeit in different cities for a span of 55 years, from the age of 22, dying while its national chairman. Appendix Five provides a samples of his itineraries, which from my limited knowledge, are just working guides.

His leadership is often cause for reminiscence. Indeed, he is often referred to in his capacity as a freedom fighter. Walls addresses this aspect when he wrote: "As chairman (Spottswood) who became deeply involved he suffers the scars of the turbulent sixties which practiced nefarious brutality against freedom lovers in defiance of justice."[148] His courageous leadership is highlighted in an editorial of the official publication of the organization, The Crisis. Quoting from a joint telegram sent to Mrs. Spottswood by the three principal officers of the NAACP upon his passing: "All his life he served his church and the NAACP even as Bishop Alexander Walters was signer of the call for the organization of the NAACP in 1909. We remember and salute his courage."[149]

147 James David Armstrong. <u>A Review of a History of John Wesley A.M.E. Zion Church, Washington D.C</u>
148 Bishop William J. Walls. <u>The African Methodist Episcopal Zion church: Reality of the Black Church.</u> (Charlotte, North Carolina: A.M.E. Zion Publishing House, 1974), p. 530
149 Crisis Editorial. "Bishop Stephen Gill Spottswood" <u>The Crisis February 1975.</u>

Spottswood was not seen by all as a fearless freedom fighter: "In the 1960's his low-key leadership of the NAACP came under criticism from more militant factions." [150] Yet others had different opinions: "While that posture might earn a younger, modern leader scant praise today, the moderation of Bishop Spottswood and men like him was the radicalism of his day."[151] Notwithstanding, he will be remembered most for his labeling the Nixon administration "anti-black." That several sources of this story could be readily had is testimony of its veracity. Indeed the Bracey and Harley (Editors) of the Papers of the NAACP put it this way, and I quote at length:

> Following the urban riots of 1967 and the widespread rioting that occurred after the assassination of Martin Luther King Jr. on April 4, 1968, the 1968 NAACP convention in Atlantic City focused on the theme of extending NAACP programs to urban ghettos and developing political and economic power in these areas. At the opening session of the convention, NAACP board chairman Stephen Gill Spottswood used his keynote address to reaffirm the NAACP's traditional commitments and to argue that the NAACP continued to be relevant to the hopes and aspirations of the majority of African Americans. Spottswood declared: "We remind America that for 59 years the NAACP has been struggling to remove the strangling inequalities of the ghetto which have stimulated the riots." He continued: "We are for the strengthening of the ghetto but not for the development of the ghetto-state.... We speak for the vast, though little publicized, majority of Negro Americans.... Inclusion is their goal, not exclusion." Other speakers at the 1968 convention offered their perspectives on the challenges

---

(NAACP), p. 41
150   African Methodist Episcopal Zion Church Conferences (New York) Sesquicentennial celebration, New York 1821-1971...From Bishop James Varick to Bishop Herbert Bell Shaw, April 24-30, 1971, (New York, NY.) p., 722
151   Ibid.

facing the NAACP and all African Americans as they sought to remedy the "urban crisis." Vivian Henderson, president of Clark College in Atlanta, Georgia, centered her remarks on the importance of employment. She recognized that the civil rights legislation of the mid-1960s was an important achievement, but she also argued that this legislation had not yet tangibly affected the lives of the majority of African Americans. She argued that employment was the best way to positively impact the lives of the residents of America's central cities. Ruth Harvey of Danville, Virginia, and Julian Bond, a former Student Nonviolent Coordinating Committee member and in 1968 a member of the Georgia House of Representatives both stressed the need for unity among African Americans and the importance of political power.

When the association met in Cincinnati, Ohio, in June 1970 for its sixty-first convention, Richard Nixon had been in the White House for about eighteen months.

The NAACP and its allies felt this was long enough to evaluate the Nixon Administration and they clearly did not like what they were seeing. Several speakers at the 1970 convention directed pointed critiques at the Nixon administration. The most controversial speech was delivered by Stephen Gill Spottswood, who began with a very brief list of some of the NAACP's accomplishments since it had last met in Cincinnati. He then quickly made his way to the heart of his speech. Spottswood declared: "For the first time since Woodrow Wilson, we have a national administration that can rightly be characterized as anti-Negro. This is the first time since 1920 that the national administration had made it a matter of calculated policy to work against the needs and aspirations of the largest minority of its citizens." Spottswood then listed nine instances of Nixon's "anti-Negro" policies, including efforts to delay school desegregation, the nominations of Clement Haynsworth and G. Harold Carswell to the Supreme Court, attempts to weaken the Voting Rights Act of 1965, and signing of defense contracts with textile companies that had records of employment discrimination. Spottswood also argued that Nixon's policies were giving encouragement to white racists. Other speakers were also critical of the Nixon administration. Leon E. Panetta questioned the administration's policies on school desegregation and NAACP Labor Department head Herbert Hill criticized the Philadelphia Plan.

Not surprisingly, the Nixon administration quickly responded to these speeches. This edition includes a telegram to Roy Wilkins from Leonard Garment, special consultant to Nixon, defending Nixon's policies. Garment argued that the Philadelphia Plan, family food assistance programs, and the naming of African Americans to policy-making positions were among some of the administration's accomplishments. Garment also argued that Spottswood misrepresented Nixon's policies in the areas of employment and school desegregation. Garment's telegram is followed by a reply from Spottswood and several other letters mentioning Spotswood's speech.[152]

Spottswood who, in July 1959, lead "the N.A.A.C.P'S twenty-two car "Freedom Train" to Washington D.C. to encourage more civil rights legislation,[153] though sorely pressed, refused to change his stance, because he felt he was standing squarely on the record of the Administration.

Though this took place in his retirement, it should be noted that he was

---

152 John H. Bracey, Jr. and Sharon Harley (Editors) Papers of the NAACP Supplement to Part 1, 1966-1970 A Microfilm Project of University Publications of America. An imprint of LexisNexis Academic Library Solutions, Bethesda, MD
153 "In The Nation's Press" quoted from The Boston Globe, Boston, Mass. December 6, 1974 in The Crisis February 1975, p. 49

still actively serving his church as Vice Chairman of the Connectional Budget Board. On the NAACP he had served in many and varied capacities, president of the Washington, D.C. Branch from 1947 to 1952, as a member of the National Board of Directors from 1955 and Chairman of its National Board of Directors on Monday, April 10, 1961, a position which he continued to served effectively until then December 1974. Appendix Six and Seven highlight the work he did while serving at the helm of that organization, leading the fight for liberation, while Appendix Eight provides a sample of one of the many sermons he preached to encourage his pastors and people.

The words of one close to him say it all: "he was extremely effective in administrative affairs...serving with tractability as publicity chairperson of the A.M.E. Zion Sesquicentennial Celebration."[154] Over the years, circumstances dictated that the Black church, especially the A.M.E. Zion Church which became known as the "Freedom Church" is the source which ensured its members took part in voter registration, which ensured its members took part in voter round-up and which ensured its members took part in getting -out-to-vote. This became a priority across the denomination if anything was to get done, even in most fortunate socio-economic, educated, groups. Indeed, the denomination joined hands with other groups in this regard. In these early twenty-first century years, while the law forbids anyone standing before a congregation and telling one's members who to vote for, one certainly has the social and political responsibility to tell and remind members to get out and vote; a responsibility that A.M.E. Zion took very seriously.

---

154 Rev. Dr. Adebola T. Odukoya. <u>Spottswood AME Zion Church: 53 Years of Faithful Testimony</u>. (Denver, Co.: Spottswood AME Zion Church, 2005), p. 15

CHAPTER SIX
BISHOP HERBERT BELL SHAW: THE IMPACT OF HIS LIFE, LEADERSHIP AND LEGACY ON THE AFRICAN METHODIST EPISCOPAL ZION CHURCH

Bishop Herbert Bell Shaw has the reputation of being strict and persistent but progressive and with a compassion for those who fell under his jurisdiction; one who was a nurturer and an expansionist at all levels. He was born in Wilmington, North Carolina, on February 9, 1908. His father was John Henry Shaw and his mother Lummie Virginia Hodges Shaw. While history does not record any siblings, his obituary did indicate he was survived by one sister, Mrs. Lucille Dudley. In a moment of foreshadowing, "he was named for a noteworthy pioneer Zion preacher in the Cape Fear Conference."[155]

A product of the public school system of Wilmington, he received his college training from Fisk University, Nashville, Tenn., where he was a student from 1924 to 1926. He attended Howard University School of Religion in Washington, D.C. from 1927 to 1928, and was awarded the honorary degree of Doctor of Divinity at Livingstone College, Salisbury, N.C."[156]

Bradley[157] tells us that young Herbert was converted in St. Luke's African Methodist Episcopal Zion Church, Wilmington, Sunday, June 13, 1920, at the

---
155   Bishop William J. Walls. <u>The African Methodist Episcopal Zion church: Reality of the Black Church.</u> (Charlotte, North Carolina: A.M.E. Zion Publishing House, 1974), p. 608
156   <u>The Obituary: Bishop Herbert Bell Shaw</u> January 7, 1980
157   David Henry Bradley, Sr. <u>A History of the A.M.E. ZION CHURH: Part II 1872-1968:</u> (Nashville: Tennessee, The Parthenon Press, 1970), p. 441.

age of about twelve. Appendix Nine provides the last sermon he delivered at his Annual Conference and it was printed in his home going program. It was while there that he was ordained a deacon on Thursday, May 10, 1928. Herbert Bell Shaw would be ordained elder two years later, on Saturday, November 15, 1930, but he would have already "returned to his home conference and (have begun to serve) as pastor ... at Bowen's Chapel, St, Andrews, and Price Memorial, in and near Wilmington, N.C."[158] Continuing to serve in the Cape Fear Conference, the Reverend Herbert Bell Shaw was appointed Presiding Elder of the Wilmington District 1937-1943.

Shaw was a preacher beloved. His efficient and effective performance of his work was noticeable to those around, and his dedication, loyalty and enthusiasm made him destined for greater things. He served the Church as Secretary-Treasurer of the Department of Home Missions, Pension and Ministerial Relief, using his skill and experience to good advantage. He held this position from 1943-1952, during which time "he helped restructure the Brotherhood pension service."[159]

The Reverend Herbert Bell Shaw was elected fifty-seventh in line of succession to the episcopacy in the African Methodist Episcopal Zion Church in 1952; first in the class of four elected that year and consecrated on Sunday, May 18 that same year.

In that capacity he served as Chairperson of the Board of Directors of the National Conference of Black Churchmen. He served as delegate to the 8th-12th World Methodist Conferences in Oxford, England (1950); Lake

---

158   Bishop William J. Walls. <u>The African Methodist Episcopal Zion church: Reality of the Black Church.</u> (Charlotte, North Carolina: A.M.E. Zion Publishing House, 1974), p. 608
159   <u>Ibid. p. 458,</u>

Junaluska, N.C. (1956); Oslo, Norway, (1961). A prolific history of service attends Bishop Shaw:

> He was a member of the General Commission of the Army and Navy Chaplains; second Vice President of the National Council of Churches of Christ in the U.S.A.; He served on a Survey Commission which traveled around the world visiting twenty-three (23) countries for the Department of Christian Education of the African Methodist Episcopal Zion Church in 1958.[160] 4-H Club of America Board of Directors; Community Boys Club of America, Wilmington, North Carolina; Omega Psi Phi Fraternity; Chair of Curriculum Committee of Department of Education; Chair.; Livingstone College Board of Trustees, Salisbury, North Carolina; Clinton Junior College, Board of Trustees, Rock Hill, South Carolina; Lomax Hannon College Board of Trustees, Greenville, Atlanta, among others. He was elected Grand Master of Prince Hall Masons of North Carolina in October 1974.[161]

Records show that as far back as 1964 he made every effort to establish an Extension School within the bounds of the New York Conference for the ministerial and lay leaders of this conference. In a letter to Bishop Shaw dated September 17, 1964, the then-Dean of the Seminary seemed enthused about the proposal himself:

> Dear Bishop Shaw: President Duncan has informed me of your interest in establishing an Extension School within the bounds of the New York Conference. Since the Extension Schools are established for the purpose of meeting the needs of the ministers and Christian lay workers within the area it is difficult or almost impossible to give one a blueprint or

---

160 Obituary, Bishop Herbert Bell Shaw
161 <u>Ibid</u> Bishop William J. Walls. <u>The African Methodist Episcopal Zion church: Reality of the Black Church.</u> (Charlotte, North Carolina: A.M.E. Zion Publishing House, 1974), p. 549

detailed plans away from the scene. In order to establish such a school it will be necessary for me to come to New York and work with persons whom you have appointed. However, there are basic policies which must be followed and adhered to as these relate to the standing of the Seminary with the accrediting association:

1. Instructors in Extension Schools must meet the same qualifications as instructors on the faculty of Hood theological Seminary. These instructors will become members of said faculty serving specifically in Extension schools.

2. Those admitted to study must meet the basic requirements for admission to Hood Theological Seminary if they wish to pursue these courses for credit.

3. A suitable place must be provided where classes may be held.

4. Transportation expenses and accommodation for teaching personnel and directors must likewise be provided.

5. Sufficient funds must be provided to pay for the services of such local persons or otherwise who may be secured to serve on the faculty and staff of the center.

6. The number of evenings per week upon which the classes are to be in session must be decided.

7. The basic fees are:

Enrollment	$5.00
Library	2.00
Tuition	12.00 per semester

Shaw was no different from the other two Bishops under consideration when it came to his interest in camp facilities. He was very supportive of the efforts of the members of the New York Conference and thus it was that "members of the New York Conference have invested in a camp in the Catskill

Mountains at Burlington, N.Y., which they named M. Ardelle Shaw Memorial Camp in honor of their missionary supervisor. Its debt was liquidated from the Sesqui-Centennial Celebration of the New York Conference in 1971."[162] 39 years have come and gone and this facility is not operational.

Bishop Shaw began his expansionist activities in his own annual conferences. Indeed, the late Reverend Dr. George W. McMurray, then pastor of the cradle of Zion Methodism, Mother A.M.E. Zion Church, New York, N.Y. took the time to write and thank his then-Presiding Prelate, Bishop Herbert Bell Shaw, for the work he was doing in this regard. Said Dr. McMurray:

June 1, 1971

Dear Bishop Shaw:

Allow me to thank you for your great work in expanding the borders of the A. M. E. Zion Church. Your work in this area and in the leadership of the church surpasses anything that I have seen during my ministerial span.

The trip to London was another revelation to us and it is unfortunate at this time that we do not have a Connectional commitment for such a program.

However, I feel that God will enable you to continue and to surround you with friends who are equally concerned with carrying the Gospel and good news to people who are waiting to receive the Message.

Enclosed ... and I pray that God will continue to bless you in your efforts. [163]

This was by no means the only person who wrote. "We had a very wonderful experience in Jamaica. If we can continue with your leadership in

---

162   Bishop William J. Walls. <u>The African Methodist Episcopal Zion church: Reality of the Black Church.</u> (Charlotte, North Carolina: A.M.E. Zion Publishing House, 1974), p.549
163   Rev. Dr. George W. McMurray, Pastor, Mother A.M.E. Zion Church, New York, New York, to Bishop Herbert Bell Shaw, 520 Red Cross Street, Wilmington, NC dated June 1, 1971

TELLING A NEGLECTED STORY

Jamaica, I am certain that we will have one of the largest and best conferences in Zion Methodism, "said Reverend Frank Jones.

Bonner in an interview stated that Bishop Shaw did not lose sight of his financial skills. "He set the agenda in getting the endowment for Livingstone College (owned by the denomination) and started an endowment fund in the New York Conference specifically to give to local churches; however with a change in administration, the funds disappeared."[164]

Throughout his years of service, Bishop Shaw was assigned to the First, Sixth, Third and Second Episcopal Districts at one time or another. Thus he was Presiding Prelate over the New York, Cape Fear, New England, Florida, West Alabama, South Carolina, Trinidad and Tobago, Jamaica, London-Birmingham, Bahamas among others.

"While assigned to the South Florida Conference, he resurrected the Bahamas Island Conference in 1950 and steered its growth during 14 years... Nine churches were reported in 1965, with a membership of 322."[165] He is also credited with reviving the work in Barbados. Hoggard noted that "Bishops Shaw and Spottswood planned to expand Zion in Barbados, where lots were purchased in Christ Church parish with the intention of erecting a Church building to the memory of Bishops John Bryan Small and Cameron Chesterfield Alleyne, both Barbadians by birth."[166]

Even as he nurtured these conferences and expanded their numbers within their borders, Shaw made new inroads in other countries. "In the

---
164   Ibid.
165   "/> Bishop William J. Walls. The African Methodist Episcopal Zion church: Reality of the Black Church. (Charlotte, North Carolina: A.M.E. Zion Publishing House, 1974), p.249
166   Bishop James Clinton Hoggard. The African Methodist Episcopal Zion Church: A Bicentennial Commemorative History (Charlotte, North Carolina: A.M.E. Zion Publishing House, 1998), P.154

1960 and early 1970s, much of the growth in overseas missions was sparked by the remarkable accomplishments of Bishop Herbert Bell Shaw...By 1972 the Jamaica Conference was one of the fastest growing conferences within the denomination. There were 177 churches, 108 pastors and an active membership of 25,750 people."[167] Persistent in his drive as an expansionist, through contacts in Jamaica, Bishop Shaw structured the London-Birmingham Conference which was officially organized May 13, 1971. His expansionist work does not end there, however, for he is also credited with bringing to fruition the Trinidad and Tobago Conference.

One could not put the drive and energy into the work as Bishop Shaw did without catching the attention of his fellow Bishops and the leadership of other Churches. As a result:

> He was Chairperson of the National Conference of Black Churchmen Board of Directors, and was Vice President, of the World Methodist Conference. He was a member of the General Commission of the Army and Navy Chaplains; second Vice President of the National Council of Churches of Christ in the U.S.A.; member of the Presidium of the World Methodist council, 1971-76; the World Council of Churches; 4-H Club of America Board of Directors; Community Boys Club of America, Wilmington, North Carolina; Omega Psi Phi Fraternity; Chair of Curriculum Committee of Department of Education; Chair, Livingstone College Board of Trustees, Salisbury North Carolina; Clinton Junior college Board of Trustees, Rock Hill, South Carolina; Lomax Hannon College Board of Trustees, Greenville, Alabama, among others. He was elected Grand Master of Prince Hall Masons of North Carolina in October, 1974.[168]

---

167 Ibid., 150
168 Ibid.,p.458

Herbert Bell Shaw was never afraid to stand on the side of right. He dared "the North Carolina Council of Churches to practice brotherhood in an address delivered at the closing session of the churchmen, held in York Auditorium Duke University."[169] Herbert Bell Shaw was an activist. Herbert Bell Shaw was a freedom fighter. In the words of one lowly minster whose eyes still look off in a distance with unspoken memories, he was a nurturer, an aggressive nurturer. Roles all seen in his Episcopal address in Appendix Ten.

---

169 Alexander Barnes. "Bishop Shaw first Race Prelate to speak at Duke" The Star Of Zion, March 5, 1959.p.1

CONCLUSION

The negative implications of the lack of available, curated resources can never be overstated; had scholars delved in this area before, that had there existed a large body of written material adding to the knowledge available to the community, the job of scholars would have been much easier, far less time consuming. There is a deep denominational neglect of the story of our past -- there is no age-old, full-fledged denominational archive, and many willing oral histories were never passed on. As a result, as one thing becomes clear, there exists a paucity of data and most definitely a rejection of the tradition and information gathered and publicized by others. In short, the challenge of African Americans in the United States continues to be shaped by the racism of a system that dominated the past. The great men and women of the past are treasured as memories and shared (informally) as oral stories, but the paper record – the documentation – is non-existent. This cannot be stated enough: this is a plea for African American congregations to make 'archives' a priority. Keep the record of the present so those in the future who want to understand where we have come from can do so.

My contribution to the literature is not intended to simply tell the story of the story of the past to satisfy curiosity, but to motivate and inspire readers especially sons and daughters of Zion, with the hope that they too will pick up the torch and ensure it burns brightly and as warmly as did John Wesley's heart. Most certainly, we must acknowledge our debt of gratitude to John and Charles

Wesley for the gift of Methodism. Their leadership in this regard continues to influence congregations around the globe and the Methodist family should take pride in the emergence of traditions such as the African Methodist Episcopal Zion Church. The African Methodist Episcopal Church (Philadelphia - Allen) and the African Methodist Episcopal Church (New York - Varick) which was later changed to African Methodist Episcopal Zion Church, two major Black Methodist denominations, started just nine years apart in different sections of the country are sister denominations that owe much of our distinctiveness to the achievements of John and Charles Wesley. We are inheritors of the Methodist tradition.

Perhaps the most important conclusion that can be drawn from this brief history is that African Americans need to write their own histories. Along the way, my readings make it very clear that Raboteau, Du Bois, Cornel West, and other scholars have rejected histories others have written, especially persons from differing racial or ethnic backgrounds and made the case for the story being told and written out of one's perspective; so too with the African Methodist Episcopal Zion Church. In the words of the current senior Bishop of the African Methodist Episcopal Zion Church, the Right Reverend George W.C. Walker, Sr.:

> Our history records our tradition. History is our record of the past. Heritage is what we presently understand about our history, which becomes our tradition. And we have a rich tradition. Our heritage has not been void of struggles. In fact, in a real sense, our struggles have given birth to our heritage. From our burdens have come our beliefs, from discrimination against us have come our determinations, from our hurts have come our hopes, from our fears have come our faith, from

our sorrows has come our songs, from our tragedies have come our triumphs; and from our oppressions have come our organization. It was important for other folk to deny our history in order to make us misunderstand our heritage and thereby eliminate our ability to produce the hopes and dreams so necessary for future generations to appreciate their tradition. They were almost successful.[170]

Analysis and language systems are key, and while research which must supplement the body of existing knowledge may be increased, such research also needs to be couched in language that documents the work of God, the liberating God, who as He did then, continues to stand ready to bring liberation to the oppressed. Our history is a history that is grounded in the action of God that liberates us from oppression. We need to think about our past so we can think about our present and future leadership. Those who make themselves available to Him for leadership must be willing like those whom we have studied, must study and work hard, to be empowered for the task.

This is a plea for inspiration. We must ask at this point; where do we go from here? Without a doubt, expansion and further research is needed. It will help put to rest some of the questions yet unanswered about the early years of Zion Methodism.

When we handle the stories of an oppressed people, we need to cultivate a certain level of postmodern sensitivity. Too often history is detached and neutral. For African Americans, too much is at stake for us to be detached and neutral. The liberation underpinnings and rejection of the history as told

---

[170] Bishop George W.C. Walker, Sr. "Revisiting the Traditions of our Fathers: Old Solutions to New Structures". The A.M.E. Zion Quarterly Review. James David Armstrong,(Editor-Manager) (Charlotte, North Carolina: 2005), pp. 4-5

by those with different eyes, lead us to its postmodern sensitivity.

Mary Ann Tolbert places this in context:

> part of the postmodern trajectory might be helpfully characterized for biblical scholars as an affirmation of radical historicity, which extends the historical consciousness of the Enlightenment to its logical end for those living in the present. If history makes us conscious that people and groups in past ages were fully situated within the cultural assumptions and conditions of their own age and were influenced into their thoughts and actions by their own distinctive social circumstances and power relations, then those same realities must of necessity condition people in contemporary societies.[171]

Tolbert takes us beyond this when she points out that "after all, the ultimate goal of all liberation movements is to change the world, and any notion, no matter how theoretical praiseworthy, that does not promote that end is useless."[172] In the opening chapter, the approach to history was described as almost pre-modern; in the conclusion, the label is postmodern. The point is that history has the power to change the present. For many African American congregations, investing resources in keeping a record of the past is a waste of resources. Such an attitude arises because history is too often viewed as simply description. History is not just description. It is a powerful tool that can change, inspire, and inform the present. There is a shared narrative among those who are studying the history of our Church that recognizes the enormous social and

---

171   Mary Ann Tolbert. "Afterward: The Politics and Poetics of Location" "Reading from this Place Volume 1: Social Location and Biblical Interpretation in the United States. Fernando F. Segovia and Mary Ann Tolbert (Editors) (Minneapolis: Fortress Press, 1995), p. 307
172   Ibid., p. 312

political implications of the emergence of the African Methodist Episcopal Zion Church. As others join the conversation, the insights that can emerge from our understanding of the past will become richer and more powerful.

Finally, standing on the shoulders of those gone before, I started out with the charge biblically, theologically and historically, to bring hope alive to Zion Methodists and others as they "keep 'agoing" for a better day, by trying to emulate Bishops Walls, Spottswood and Shaw. It seems clear to me, however, that much work yet remains to be done; an oral history and six official history books are desperately insufficient for the task of communicating decades of contentious history.

This is a beginning. Other ways need to be found to tell the story of these remarkable men and women who shaped our tradition, and most importantly, others need to be inspired by the story of our past to serve effectively in the present.

APPENDICES

CYNTHIA STEWART

APPENDIX ONE

COPY

December 31, 1959

Dear Brother:

You have not written me on how you have started off. You have one of the best appointments near the college for a student to get, but 1 am afraid you do net appreciate it.

I know that you are spending a lot of energy trying to borrow money from credit unions around Salisbury and Hickory. I would suggest that, as you have a furnished parsonage and a stated salary, that you ad- just yourself to your income and use some patience by waiting: until you have grown in your own situation; and if you owe debts, it is better to owe them where they are than to make new debts.

I must ask that you cease to give my name as reference for borrowing money because I will have to deny it, and if you find that the church does not pay enough for your living obligations and going to school, I suggest that you give it up rather than to heap up debts and have you and the church embarrassed in the long run. You can get pretty nice Jobs up this way if you are not willing to wait on your growth in the church.

Somehow you make me have deep concern and create doubts about the type of servant of God you are going to make as a preacher when you show such restlessness and such looseness in your financial ambition.

To me, you are in a big hurry and want to live too fast. If your wife is prodding: you, tell her to give you time and you will make a much better husband in the future if she does not crush you with demands in the present.

I wish you growing success, and I shall expect to see you when I come down.

Very truly yours

W.J . WALLS

APPENDIX TWO

Report

to the

Harriet Tubman Home Board of Directors

Hyatt Regency Hotel

Old Greenwich, CT

October 7, 2009

PROGRESS REPORT

Harriet Tubman Bronze Memorial Plaque Project

December 2007 the HTH Board voted to commission sculptures of Harriet Tubman. Last year at the 2008 General Conference, the HTH announced the Limited Edition Harriet Tubman Bronze Memorial Plaque Project chaired by HTH board member and Missionary Supervisor, Mrs. Iris M. Battle. Mrs. Battle and the HTH Board are gratified by the response to this project. Many different parts of Zion responded favorably to this effort including the Board of Bishops. Bishop and Mrs. Battle and the HTH Board lift up the example of the YPC of the Western New York Conference who purchased a Harriet Tubman Bronze Memorial Plaque as a gift to President and Mrs. Obama and Malia and Sasha. There are a few remaining of this limited edition Tubman Plaque available for purchase for $500.00. We respectfully request that all unfulfilled pledges for the plaque be completed at this time. Remember the sculpture initiative is a two part project. HTH must complete the sales of the plaque in order to move forward with the sculpting of the life size statue of Harriet Tubman to be installed at the home site.

Tubman Home Site Activities

The HTH continues to conduct historical cultural tours for a diverse audience of visitors. Visitation remains stable and constant in spite of continued high fuel costs and the state of the economy overall. The HTH remains affordable with adult admission, $5.00 and children and seniors, $3.00. The HTH is on target to receive approximately 5000-6000 visitors by yearend.

The HTH has been working with the New York State office of Parks, Recreation and Historic Preservation in several areas including developing new ways to enhance the visitor experience through interpretation of the site and its exhibits. This work has evolved over a two year period and the draft tour script in under review (see attached). This is an important element for Tubman as the tour provides the narrative voice to support the unique features of the home site and must be consistently delivered to a diverse public. In addition to the script and its notes, testing and training of existing staff is a part of what will be required in order to qualitatively improve tour operations. With current fiscal crisis in New York, the Harriet Tubman Home remains one of three sites receiving consultant resources from the state.

The preservation construction of the Tubman Barn is near complete. The work on the Tubman residence is scheduled to commence in the coming weeks to be followed by the completion of the basement and second floor of the Home for the Aged established by Harriet Tubman, as per the specifications previously shared. A schedule of expenditures is attached.

The unforeseen delays due to archaeological and environmental factors required the Crawford and Stearns, the federally approved preservation planners to revise the construction timeline. Significant archaeological artifacts were discovered including a cistern. Environmentally the HTH has been contaminated by the presence of two underground fuel tanks embedded by the Norris Family, a onetime owner of the Tubman residence. The HTH is responsible for cleaning the site and will determine if it has any legal recourse in this matter. NYS Department of Environmental Conservation is working cooperatively with the HTH. Pursuant to a meeting of the HTH Executive Committee, the HTH entered into a Stipulation with the NYSDEC to clean the contamination. The environmental technologies firm of Eisenbach and Ruhnke has been retained to manage the plans to clean the contamination caused by the fuel spill. Stipulation and Eisenbach and Ruhnke Agreement are attached.

Harriet Tubman Special Resource Study and Legislation – S.227 and HR1078

The advocacy of the HTH under Bishop Battle's leadership has been tremendous and effective. The HTH challenged the Department of the Interior's National Park Service (NPS) to give full recognition to the AME Zion, privately owned Auburn site. As all are aware, the NPS was commissioned in 2000 to provide the United States Congress with the Harriet Tubman Special Resource Study (SRS) to determine:

> If Harriet Tubman's accomplishment were sufficiently significant to warrant national recognition; and

> If yes to the above referenced, then what would be the most appropriate manner to honor and preserve Tubman's historical contributions

Encountering initially a hostile, hyper-critical and biased environment with the NPS, the HTH soldiered on to overcome the obvious NPS support for the Maryland sites to the diminishment of Tubman in Auburn, New York. Indeed the SRS was delayed four years in its release while the NPS spent time, energy and resources to make the case for the Maryland sites. This delay has served to the detriment of the already up and running Auburn site to receive federal resources to assist with the maintenance and upkeep of the site. Moreover the SRS was clearly biased in giving Maryland more prominence in the report. The rationale; the SRS will also serve as the basis for Maryland to receive a Statement of Significance (SOS) which is a prerequisite for any consideration of a further relationship between Maryland and the NPS. The HTH received its SOS in 1987.

The HTH did ultimately prevail on all important issues in the SRS. The SRS does recommend that the HTH become a national historical park thus enabling it to be eligible for the maximum in funding allocations from the NPS. Most importantly the SRS and all proposed legislation makes clear the continued exclusive private ownership of the HTH by the African Methodist Episcopal Zion Church as a fundamental component of the Auburn, New York Tubman site. The HTH has been persistent yet collegial in negotiating with the NPS as evidenced by the HTH hosting, on short notice, the second public meeting on the SRS. .

The 110th U.S. Congress closed prior to taking up the Tubman legislation. It is viewed as a priority by the bill's sponsors therefore it was introduced early in the 111th U.S. Congress by Senator Benjamin Cardin with the full support of the bills co-sponsors. The current legislation is indexed as S.227 in the Senate and HR. 1078 in the House of Representatives. The sponsor of the House bill is Rep. Michael Arcuri of the 24th Congressional District which includes Auburn, New York. HR.1078 has fifty two co-sponsors and is co-incident in large measure with the Senate bill. The Senate bill was introduced with unanimous consent. S.227 is attached.

Congressional Hearings on Tubman Legislation

The Harriet Tubman Home was invited to testify on behalf of HR 1078 to establish the Harriet Tubman National Historical Park in Auburn, New York and the Harriet Tubman Underground Railroad National Historical Park in Caroline, Dorchester and Talbot Counties in Maryland before the House Sub-Committee on National Parks, Forests and Public Lands on March 24, 2009. The written and oral testimonies were well received by Rep. Grijalva, Chairman. There were three important points raised in the testimony. They were as follows:

The Name of the Auburn, New York Tubman Park - The Harriet Tubman Home and the AME Zion Church request that the name of the Auburn, New York site is changed to the "Harriet Tubman Home National Historical Park" The Harriet Tubman Home in Auburn, New York is the place where Ms. Tubman spent more than five decades of her life. It is the only place in the world with the extant resources which documents Tubman's life and contributions to her community and America;

Inclusion of Tubman Barn as a Contributing Property - The Harriet Tubman Home and its consultant preservation architects and planners consider the Tubman Barn a contributing building on the property in addition to the buildings and sites referenced as "nationally significant resources" in H.R. 1078. The Barn was constructed under Harriet Tubman's ownership c. 1896. The barn is currently undergoing restoration; and most importantly

Rationale for Modifying Matching Funds Requirement -The Harriet Tubman Home and the AME Zion Church have been responsible and sacrificial stewards of the Tubman property for more than 105 years, keeping the assembled parcel intact because of a collective and unshakable belief that America would one day honor Harriet Tubman's service to her country in the Freedom Movement which includes her military service and her humanitarian ethos. The ability to keep the assembled parcel intact for over 105 has not been without severe financial and human resource struggle. It would not have been possible without the contributions of former slaves and their descendents. This commitment to not let Harriet Tubman's legacy die has led the Auburn, New York Tubman home site to be open year round, providing historic cultural tours to approximately eight thousand visitors annually, the majority of whom, are students.

The full written testimony of the March 24, 2009 hearing is attached. On Wednesday, July 15, the United States Senate Subcommittee on held hearings on the S.227, The testimony submitted by the Harriet Tubman Home in the House of Representatives was used for establishing the record for the Auburn, New York site since there were no objections or concerns regarding the previously submitted written testimony. At the outset of the hearing Senator Udall, Chairman boldly proclaimed that there is complete support in the Committee on Energy and Natural Resources Subcommittee on National Parks to establish the Harriet Tubman National Historical Park in Auburn, New York and the Harriet Tubman Underground Railroad National Historical Park in Caroline, Dorchester and Talbot Counties in Maryland.

Funding Arc and Advocacy to Support Tubman Park

Initially, the NPS did not support a steady stream of funding to the Harriet Tubman Home because of the insistence that the property remained exclusively owned by the AME Zion Church. Through the persistence of the HTH, the

NPS changed its position and a preservation easement is being negotiated. The preservation easement originally was to be "granted" to the NPS. The HTH through its effective advocacy on behalf of the AME Zion Church and the Harriet Tubman Home will be compensated for the preservation easement. This will be in addition to the funding cited on the current proposed legislation.

The legislation introduced in June 2008 proposed 7.5 million for the HTH. The 7.5 million represented a considerable amount of interface with the NPS to reach this level (the NPS originally considered significantly lower funding for the HTH and no recognition as a national historical park). Under the leadership of Bishop Battle, letters were drafted to Sen. Clinton and Sen. Schumer to discuss parity in the legislation for the Auburn site and related deficiencies identified in the legislation.

In addition to the legislative issues to be conquered the HTH has to continue to interface with the NPS regarding the SRS and its required processes which included two public meetings in Auburn, New York to assess public opinion and the presentation of the draft results and recommendations of the study. Diverse public sentiment overwhelmingly supported the establishment of the Harriet Tubman National Historical Park in Auburn along with support that the Auburn site receives adequate resources.

The draft SRS was released November 19, 2008 for a 30 day public comment. Bishop Battle marshaled a comprehensive and credible response to the yearend release of the much overdue significant report that the country would use to determine both the form and substance for how America would honor the life of Harriet Tubman. The HTH was effective in having the NPS accept petitions from the HTH and the AME Zion Church as opposed to having to mount a campaign for the transmittal of individual comment letters. Ergo, the HTH critiqued the draft SRS and crafted petitions to respond to the most critical areas of concern. The primary areas of concern were as follows:

- ☐ Recognition that the HTH has the only extant resources in the world where Tubman's life can be documented;
- ☐ Sufficient financial resources to support the park and financial resources to support the exploration of Tubman's contemporary relevance;
- ☐ Financial support for a Conference/Interpretive Center;
- ☐ Immediate financial support for daily operations at the HTH;
- ☐ Compensation for the proposed Preservation Easement;
- ☐ The HTH will have a Park Superintendent exclusively assigned to the Auburn site;
- ☐ Reduction in the matching funds requirement for the HTH in

- recognition of the 100 plus years of responsible stewardship by the AME Zion Church; and
- ☐ In citing the core values of Tubman, the report fails to cite Tubman's core belief of the presence of God in her life along with her long time membership in the Thompson Memorial AME Zion Church and the acknowledgement that the local church was a part of the connectional AME Zion Church, known historically as the "Freedom Church".

The technical content and import of Bishop Battle's letter is discussed below. Bishop Battle wrote a strong letter of support on behalf of the Auburn, New York site and the sacrifices of the AME Zion church in maintaining the HTH. Bishop Battle most importantly recommended that the NPS issue a FONSI (Finding of No Significant Impact) as required by the Environmental Protection Agency, thus allowing the HTH to become a national historical park. The NPS was so overwhelmed by the volume of responses regarding the HTH coming from the AME Zion Church and friends of the HTH that they had to come into their offices on the weekend in order to properly quantify the responses to the draft SRS study. Bishop Battle's letter and sample petitions are attached.

The results of the above referenced actions has resulted in the legislation introduced in the 111th Congress which increases the funding allocation for the HTH from 7.5 million to 11 million, in addition the HTH will have a cooperative agreement of $200,000 annually with Livingstone College to advance scholarly work on the life of Harriet Tubman. And as previously cited there will be consideration for Preservation Easement, estimated to bring as much as an additional 3 million to the AME Zion Church and the HTH.

President Barack Obama will be signing the Tubman legislation. All sponsors are working very hard to have this legislation make its way through the Senate and the House of Representatives in this session of Congress. Clearing the Senate subcommittee was a huge step forward for the HTH. The Senate and House will now move to conference on the nearly identical bills and vote out the proposed legislation to establish the Harriet Tubman National Historical Park in Auburn, New York and Maryland. We are working with our Maryland counterparts to support a bill signing event preferably in Washington, DC since both the Eastern Shore of Maryland and Auburn, New York may be considered too remote. All are encouraged to write their United States Senators and members of the subcommittee in support of the bill and the three concerns of the HTH.

The additional resources to HTH may be used to accelerate the campaign and construction of a conference facility and interpretive center on the property across the road from the HTH.

Maryland Visit

Building on the early leadership of Bishop Walker in sojourning from Maryland to Auburn, New York, a delegation of HTH board members selected by Bishop Battle visited the Maryland sites over the course of two days to examine Tubman's environment in her early years (although no sites could be documented) and determine meaningful ways in with the sites could work cooperatively as an element of conducting the due diligence as the HTH moves toward national historical park status. The Maryland effort is expected to be open to the public in 2013, whereas Auburn is up and running have calendared 106 years of stewardship of Tubman's home site for more than five decades of her life

APPENDIX THREE

ONE OF OUR SIGNIFICANT LETTERS FROM DR. KING.

Southern Christian Leadership Conference
334 Auburn Ave., N.E.
Atlanta, Georgia 20302
Telephone 522-1420

Martin Luther King, Jr., President   Ralph Abernathy, Treasurer
Andrew J. Young, Executive Director

January 30, 1967 Bishop W. J. Walls

First Episcopal District
4736 South Parkway
Chicago, Illinois 60615

Dear Bishop Walls:

I wanted personally to thank you for your generous contribution to the Southern Christian Leadership Conference.

I often wish our loyal contributors could know more directly how important their support is to us, how decisive it has been in changing appalling conditions in the nation. Only ten years ago Negroes in the South lived with bruising humiliation and hopelessness.   Everything meaningful in education, employment, culture, self-government and recreation was barred to him by the cruelest custom and institutionalized mechanisms.   The vast changes our struggles created with your support have opened a new life for millions.

A complete solution has not yet been achieved but an inspiring beginning has been made and the road ahead is clearly defined.   We know that there will be many setbacks before us, but our shackled past is behind us.   The knowledge that we can count on warm friends is a continuing source of strength and confidence.

I know that you cannot enjoy the experience of change as we who see it firsthand every day, but I trust that these few words can convey our gratitude and appreciation.

With warmest personal regards, I am, Sincerely yours.

Martin Luther King, Jr.

TELLING A NEGLECTED STORY

Victim of Envy, Slain by Talent

By William Jacob Walls

(EDITOR'S NOTE: *The following article is a re-print from the January 18, 1923 issue of The Star of Zion. Bishop William Jacob Walls was editor of The Star at that time.*)

In an extensive discussion of Marcus Garvey, Dr. DuBois has made the observation that the African leader had taken a fallout with each of his cabinets annually, and had continuously changed the personnel of his chief men. We remember then that Reverend J. W. H. Eason, who had been chaplain general from the incipiency of the organizations and so kept the audiences at Liberty Hall thrilled when Mr. Garvey was absent, was selected two and a half years ago the First American leader in the enlarged program, was successful in weathering all the storms and retaining the favor of the chief.

But we reckoned too early there was a cruel fate in the background for Eason. He was elected with a popular vote for four years, and next to Garvey, was the most popularly known member of the movement. He toured the United States from east to west and with this deep-toned, musical voice, his great Indian-like head, his magnetic manners, his wit and humor, and his unusual memory and resourceful speech that gave him a carrying eloquence which no audience could resist, embraced fully the Garvey propaganda, and planted the U.N.I.A. in hundreds of cities from coast to coast.

Where he traveled, a bodyguard attended and protected him. He was regarded an exemplary leader until two events: namely, the collapse of the Black Star Line projects and the visit of Mr. Garvey to the Imperial Wizard of the Ku Klux Klan, Mr. Williams J. Simmons. Eason was in the far west and telegraphed in New York that the visit was a blunder and would give trouble on the field unless some good explanation was forth-coming. It was known that he and other leaders felt that some set-back would come from the loose business methods in handling the Black Star Line, but still Dr. Eason defended that U.N.I.A. He separated the projects and explained that the failure of the Black Star Line had nothing to do with the U.N.I.A. He was as loyal a Garveyite as anybody has found. He differed with his best friends for Mr. Garvey. We have heard him say that Garvey had the only program for the Negro and our only hope was in the movement.

But when he asserted his ideas in helping by criticism within, and some division of opinion began to arise, Mr. Garvey and his close followers rose up and made charges, which the trial of Eason failed to establish. The U.N.I.A. Court at the last New York Convention failed to convict Eason. Mr. Garvey then carried it to the convention floor and using the steamroller method, had the meeting vote Eason's expulsion for 99 years.

Eason and friends proceeded to organize another group with Garvey idea for Americans, except that the African redemption idea was dropped. There was some bitterness and Eason was constantly warned, threatened and attacked for his strong anti-Gravey [sic] speeches. It was feared that he being a competent leader in the movement from the beginning would do great harm. But Eason was determined. He had not a drop of cowardice in his blood, and when he once set is head, he was inflexible.

Immediately before leaving New York for New Orleans for the Emancipation address, which he was assassinated. He received a letter telling him that he would never live to appear at the trial of Mr. Garvey and the Black Star Line promoters. He was persuaded by close friends, schoolmates and church people to keep close and not go south for the big Emancipation demonstration. But he said he feared nobody. He must have meant it. For after his speech, he was standing carelessly in the crowd in front of the church when leaving the anti-Gravey [sic] meeting. In such a bitter fight, and with race fanaticism running so high as he knew things to be, and after a brave, and no doubt, bitter speech in which he denounced Garvey as a menace, it looked like suicidal carelessness to have gone out into the promiscuous crowd. In New York, where William Pickens held anti-Garvey meetings last summer, there were lines of policemen, and the speakers were all protected. Dr. Eason was, we think, not wise in his lack of precaution, when it is remembered that another attempt had been made upon his life, and that he received letters about the very affair and occasion.

The press account of the shooting say: "On leaving the church, with the streets crowded with persons, two shots rang out in the stillness of the night air. As the lecturer slowly sank to the ground, three persons were seen to slink quietly away. A crowd immediately gathered. Reverend Eason was rushed to the Charity Hospital where it was discovered that one bullet had struck him in the head above the right eye, and another had entered his back. After hovering between life and death four days, the Former Garvey leader died."

He identified nobody, but members of the crowd did, and William Shakespeare and Fred Dyer were arrested. Shakespeare is chief of the police in the U.N.I.A. There witnesses positively identified them as Eason's assailants.

Reverend Eason made the startling charge that orders had gone down from New York, "to put me out of the way, and prevent my appearing as a witness against Marcus Garvey at the trial to be held this week." It is all too sad Eason is gone, but what will be the outcome? This paper makes no charge. The Negro World charges Eason as dying with a lie on his lips and indicts his character seriously. We rise to protests. Eason did not lie. He quoted the threatening letter he had received. It is perfectly believable. Whether he was correct or not is another matter. The courts will help out here. Eason was not a perfect man nor are any of his accusers. But J.W. Hood Eason did not deserve to be killed. He was bold, he was persistent, he was gullible and even willful. But he was a Christian. He did not harm. Sometimes bitter in speech and a strong opponent when he took a fallout with one, but he was a trained Christian from a plain old North Caroline home, and one of the noted families of Sunbury, where he was born thirty-seven (37) years ago. He was trained at Livingstone College where he went on to prepare for the ministry. He entered on the Second High School Class and finished College in 1909, and the Theology Department in 1914. He was christened by Bishop J.W. Hood with the old sire's name given him, and bore it with talent and influence.

There never came a boy to Livingstone College with such trained eloquence from the first. In an election of the annual commencement Literary Society orator, which the students selected young Eason, while new in school, startled and carried that house in an impromptu speech, which we never heard equaled as an impromptu by a student in any college.

He was born with unusual gifts, and in Charlotte, Concord, Fayetteville and Philadelphia, no ex-pastor could call out a more enthusiastic and admiring audience when he visited his ex-parish. He secured for Zion the Metropolitan Church at Philadelphia where Rev. C.C. Williams pastors, and where Dr. C.S. Whitted has protected it for the denomination. He had arranged to take charge of a new congregation on New York and Bishop Caldwell had rented a hall looking forward to a substantion organization with him as a leader. He would have preached in that hall the Sunday following his death in New York. He had arranged with his wife before going to New Orleans to have her with him in a definition [service in his new field, and gradually, he told the bishop, he would get back into the active ministry of his own Zion. But he was cut short.]

APPENDIX FIVE

Schedule: Stephen Gill Spottswood, 1931 16th Street, N.W. Washington 9, D. C.

Telephone. DEcatur 2-7358   January 16 to March 3, 1958

Sat.   Jan. 18- Lv Washington, 5.40 P.M. B&O tr #19

Sun.   Jan. 19- Ar Detroit, Mich, 7.50 A.M. C/o Rev. T. A. Hilliard, 690 West Chicago Blvd. Telephone TOwnsend 8-2957

    11 A.M. St Paul's Church, Dr. W.A. Hilliard, Pastor

    4 P.M. Tea-Temple B'Nai Moshe

Mon.   Jan. 20- Lv. Detroit 7.50 A.M., Wacash tr #1

    Ar. St. Louis, Mo, 4.25 P.M.

Tues.   Jan. 21-Lv. St. Louis, 5.45 P.M. M-P, tr #1

    Ar. Little Rock, Ark. 12.30 A.M. C/o Mr. Milton Cannon, 1014 Pulaski St., Telephone: FRanklin

    4-2578 To Warren, Ark. C/o Rev. S.P. Spottswood, P.O. Drawer 151, Telephone, 1420

Wed.   Jan. 22-

Thurs. Jan. 23- Lv. Little Rock, 12.35 A.M., M.P. tr #21

    Ar. Houston, Texas, 10.40 A.M. – C/o Mr. J.E. Robinson, 2413 Dowling St., Telephone: FAirfax 3-3095

    11 A.M. Texas Conference Founders Day Check-up Meeting, Walls Chapel, Rev. H.G. Tillman Pastor

    8 P.M. Special Service, Walls Chapel

Fri.   Jan. 24- Lv. Houston, 4.15 P.M. M.P tr #22

Sat.   Jan. 25- Ar. St. Louis, Mo. 8.25 A.M.

    Lv. St. Louis, Mo. 8.25 A.M.

    Ar. Kankakee, Ill., 1.30 P.M. C/o Rev. John W. Frazier, 390 E. Water St. Telephone, 2-2054

TELLING A NEGLECTED STORY

Sun.	Feb. 9- 11 A.M. Greater Walters Church, Rev. N.L. Meeks, Pastor
	Lv. Chicago, 4 P.M. N.Y.C. tr #68
Mon.	Feb. 10- Ar. New York, N.Y., 9 A.M. C/o N.A.A.C.P., 20 West 40th Street, Telephone LOngacre 3-6890
	Lv. New York City, 6.25 P.M., Pa. tr #151
Tues.	Feb. 11- Ar. Salisbury, N.C., 7.15 A.M., C/o Livingstone College; Telephone 1400
	11 A.M. and 4 P.M., Board of Bishops Meetings
Wed.	Feb. 12- Livingstone College Founders' Day-Bd. Bishops Mtgs.
Thurs.	Feb. 13- Lv. Salisbury 8.25 P.M., So. Tr #38
Fri.	Feb. 14- Ar. Washington, D.C. 4.20 A.M. Off at 7.30 A.M.
Wed.	Feb. 19- Lv. Washington, 10.00 PM, B&O tr #17
Thurs.	Feb. 20- Ar. Cleveland, Ohio, 8.45 AM C/o Rev. A.L. Fuller 10,915 Fuller Ave, Telephone GLenville 1-0847
	11 AM- Columbus District Missionary Mass Meeting,
	Emmanu-El Church, Rev. C.C. Ware, Pastor
Fri.	Feb. 21- Lv. Cleveland, 8.15 AM, N.Y.C. tr #75
	Ar. Toledo, Ohio, 10.20 AM C.o Rev. W.C. Ardrey,
	954 Belmont Ave, Telephone , CHerry 6-2578
Sat.	Feb. 22- Lv. Toledo, 12.38 AM, Pa. tr #464
	Ar. Pittsburgh, Pa., 7.25 AM To Aliquippa, Pa;
	C/o Rev. W.P. Dockery, 183 6th Ave; Telephone ESsex 5-9460
Sun.	Feb. 23- 11 AM Emmanu-El Church, Rev. W.P. Dockery, pastor
Mon.	Feb. 24- Lv. Pittsburgh, 8.25 P.M. Pa. tr #33
Tues.	Feb. 25- Ar. St. Louis, Mo, 7.15 A.M.
	Lv. St. Louis, Mo, 8.55 A.M. Wa. Tr #3
	Ar. Columbia, Mo., 12.05 P.M. C/o Chaplain J.E. Williams, 203 West Ash

Sun.	Jan. 26- 11A.M. Caldwell Chapel, Rev. J.W. Frazier, Pastor
	Lv. Chicago 4.30 P.M., B&C tr #6
Mon.	Jan. 27- Ar. Washington, D.C., 8.50 A.M.
Sat.	Feb. 1- Lv. Washington, 3.00 P.M., Pa. tr #170
	Ar. North Philadelphia 5.12 P.M.
	Lv. North Philadelphia, 6.19 P.M., Pa. tr #31
Sun.	Feb. 2- Ar. Indianapolis, Indiana, 7.25 A.M., C/o Rev. E.X. Kenney, 1944 Highland Place; Telephone: WAlnut 6-5591
	11 A.M. Jones Tabernacle, Rev. E.X. Kenney, Pastor
Mon.	Feb. 3- Indiana Conference Founders Day Check-up Meeting, Alleyne Chapel, Rev. M.E. Johnson, Pastor
	Lv. Indianapolis, 10.35 P.M. N.Y.C. tr #408
Tues.	Feb. 4- Ar. Cleveland, Ohio, 5.22 A.M. – Off at 7.30 A.M. C/o Rev. A.L. Fuller, 10,915 Drexel Ave: Telephone, GLenville 1-0847
	11 A.M. Ohio Conference Founders Day Check-up Meeting, St. Paul's Church, Rev. A.L. Fuller, Pastor – To Akron Wed. Feb. 5
Wed.	Feb. 5- C/o Rev. E.E. Morgan, Jr. 799 Diagonal St. Akron, Ohio, Telephone, Blackstone 3-2567
	8 P.M. Ordination Service-Wesley Temple, Rev. E.E. Morgan, Pastor.
Thurs.	Feb. 6- Lv. Akron, 2.45 A.M., B&O tr #19
	Ar. Detroit, Mich, 7.50 A.M. C/o Dr. W.A. Hilliard, 690 West Chicago Blvd: Telephone: TOwnsend
	8-2957
Fri.	Feb.7- Lv. Detroit 11.59 A.M., N.Y.C. tr #315
	Ar. Chicago, 7.05 A.M. (La Salle Street Station) C/o Rev. N.L. Meeks, 4444 South Ellis Ave; Telephone, ATlantic 5-4196
	11 A.M. Chicago District Founders Day Checkup Meeting, Blackwell Memorial Church, Rev. W.T. Beck, Pastor
	8 P.M. "Founders Day Banquet" Blackwell Memorial Church

Street

Wed.	Feb. 26- Lv. Columbia, 4.35 P.M. Wa. Tr #9	
Thurs.	Feb. 27- Ar. Denver, Colorado, 8.05 A.M. C/o Mrs. Susie Mallard, 2338 Clarkson Street, Telephone TAbor 5-8952	
To		
Sun.	Mar. 2- Colorado Conference, Spottswood Church, Rev. C.J. Howell, Pastor	
	Lv. Denver, 4.15 P.M., D&RGW tr #12	
Mon.	Mar. 3- Ar. St. Louis, 12.30 P.M. M.P. tr #12	
Tues.	Mar. 4- Ar. North Philadelphia, 7.40 A.M.	
	Lv. North Philadelphia, 7.59 A.M. Pa tr #131	
	Ar. Washington, 10.20 A.M. or 12.10 P.M.	

APPENDIX SIX

Keynote Address at the 52nd Annual Convention of the National Association for the Advancement of Colored People, by the Chairman of the National Board of Directors, the Rt. Rev. Stephen Gill Spotswood, Philadelphia, Pa., Monday, July 10, 1961, 8:30 P.M. At Tindley Temple ME Church, Broad and Fitzwater Streets.

FREEDOM - THE NEW FRONTIER

Mr. Chairman, President Spingarn, Mr. Wilkins, fellow-directors, distinguished platform guests, members of the 52nd Annual Convention of the National Association for the Advancement of Colored People, ladies and gentlemen.

Keenly conscious of the great honor which is mine tonight, to address you as chairman of your National Board of Directors, and equally aware of the great responsibility which is mine in being assigned the task of sounding a keynote for this convention, I trust that I may leave you at least one thought which will be of constructive inspiration.

All Americans, regardless of party affiliation, were challenged by the suggestion of President Kennedy, in his acceptance speech in Los Angeles last July, that we would advance upon new frontiers. Having overcome the geographical frontiers of much of this continent, it was logical to suggest that the civic, economic, educational, health and social problems of the mid-twentieth century constituted new frontiers for courageous and resourceful Americans to overcome.

Tonight I wish to submit that among the frontiers yet remaining Is one that continues to challenge all America and the rest of the world. Freedom Is the old and the ever-new frontier 1 We cannot advance to the idealistic possibilities and the realistic necessities of the democracy conceived in the Constitution and Bill of Rights until we have climbed the mountains, bridged the rivers and carved roads through the wilderness of our American life to reach the goal of full freedom for all our citizens.

Fifty-two years ago the founders of the National Association for the Advancement of Colored People chose to pioneer through the maelstrom of our discriminatory democracy and segregated Americanism and make all our people economically free from serfdom, educationally free from segregation and socially free from discrimination.

Twenty-one years ago we met in convention here in Philadelphia. That convention had 400 delegates from 33 states. This 1961 convention has 1,200 delegates as of this afternoon, from 44 states.

In that year - 1940 - the NAACP had 50,556 members in 352 adult

Branches. For 1960 the total was 388,000 members in 1,425 Branches, Youth Councils and College Chapters.

Aside from our own NAACP growth, one dramatic development illustrates the changes that have been wrought in the onslaught against racial proscription. When we met in 1940, the United States Air Corps (as It was known then) was completely lily-white. In fact, responsible officials in the military establishment were debating soberly whether the Negro was capable of flying an airplane I On June 15 last year, an Air Force jet, the tanker version of the Boeing 707, was flown 7,175 miles non-stop from Japan to North Carolina In 12 1/2 hours with a Negro captain from Albany, Georgia, at the controls.

Tonight we do not rely on this one incident as a measure of progress, satisfying though It Is. Nor do we of the NAACP content ourselves with the history (though glorious) of the struggles of years far in the past. Sure-footed and solidly-based progress is achieved not through occasional spectacular forays, but through unrelenting and unceasing pressure on all fronts across the years, in every year.

Thus we Shall not only the events of 1940, but those of the twelve months since our last convention in St. Paul. Our Youth Council in Durham, N. C, opening up new employment In 29 stores of that city. Our Minnesota State Branches successfully sponsoring the enactment of a fair housing law. Our student Chapters at Tugaloo College and Jackson State College In Mississippi being jailed for challenging a Lily-white "public" library and segregated city buses.

Our Tampa, Fla., Branch adding 4,000 names to the voter list. Our Reno-Sparks, Nev., Branch securing the elimination of discrimination in public places. Our Oklahoma City, Okla., Youth Council winning only last week a four-year sit-in campaign against the city's largest department store. The splendid Lockheed Aircraft Corporation case In which our documented complaints and demands brought about an agreement between the corporation and the President's Committee on Equal Job Opportunity, which will result In opening up thousands of jobs In plants over the nation which hold government contracts. The 18-month trade-withholding campaign of our Savannah, Ga., Branch.

The continuing work of our Los Angeles Branch on the problem of employment and roles in the films and in television. The sit-in and other demonstrations against segregation by our young people in Kentucky, Tennessee, South Carolina and Arkansas. The work of our branches in Texas, Georgia, Pennsylvania, North Carolina and New York In the area of school desegregation. And just a week ago - the victorious climax to the long campaign of our Illinois Branches for a state FEP law.

THE FIGHT IS ON

Despite these successes and those monumental ones of other years, we know that the fight is still on! Freedom constitutes a new frontier because it is only partially won. Perhaps its loftiness is the reason why it presents difficulties of frontier proportions. The American pioneer was forced to proceed at ox-cart pace. He literally had to carve a road out of the wilderness.

He had to find passage through mountain ranges. He had to stop to build bridges when he reached the rivers. Sometimes he hewed logs and built boats to use the streams as a pathway in order to proceed on his journey to physical freedom and economic security.

Today we live in a jet <u>age</u>. We are not content with the slow pace of the ox-cart, the

faster gait of the horse and buggy, the accelerated speed of the automobile, or even the limited flight of the DC-3. Today's six hundred-miles-per-hour travel merely presages tomorrow's missile-propelled, atomic-powered propulsion-car of the twenty-first Christian century, bridging Washington and Accra in half an hour. Therefore, we must find ways to accelerate the pace of on-coming democracy.

Our program, no longer confined to battles for separate-but-equal accommodations and facilities, advanced above any doubt as to the constitutional validity of our premise, is now above the clouds and must proceed with supersonic speed, to save our society from plunging into communistic socialism and to link the world's continents in an endless chain of true democracy for all citizens of the one-world of the future.

Freedom's supersonic aircraft is <u>delayed</u> for her long-awaited takeoff by various forces which are cited in St. Paul's Ephesians (Eph. 6: 12) exhortations: "For we wrestle not against flesh and blood, but against principalities, against powers, against that rulers of the darkness of this world, against spiritual wickedness in high places."

The White Citizens Councils, the Ku Klux Klan, the Southern Gentlemen, Inc., some Southern Governors, and, lately, the John Birch Society, to name a few, illustrate one type of traffic delaying our flight to freedom.

The brutal mob action of the Ku Klux Klan in Alabama against the Freedom Riders this spring shocked the entire nation, including some daily newspapers in Alabama. Governor John Patterson of Alabama, the state where a bus was burned and where black and white men and women were set upon and beaten by race-hating hoodlums while police turned their backs, tried to speak of states' rights to his fellow Governors at a conference in Hawaii. He talked, but he reached nobody because the mob had spoken to them so loudly long before\

The "warnings" of Governor Patterson and his kind of states' righter's will fall on deaf ears as long as they encourage and condone barbaric mob assaults on the low level of race. No Governor of a non-Southern state, however he may view Federal action in certain areas, will knowingly align himself with the monstrous states' wrongs perpetrated against the Freedom Riders by Alabama in the name of the states' rights. The virulence of the Alabama disease is attested to by the extraordinary fact that even Mississippi refused to follow the bloody example of Montgomery and Birmingham.

In a way, the newly-revealed John Birch Society is more of a threat than iron-pipe mobsters in Alabama, for the Birch Society wears the robes of respectability and does not conduct its campaigns in gutters and alleys. But do not be deceived. Its No. 1 objective is the impeachment of Chief Justice Earl Warren of the United States Supreme Court for handing down the school segregation ruling.

The Birch Society is also against Federal civil rights action and for leaving such matters to the states. Finally, the Birch Society believes in restricting voting rights to those who, in its judgment, are "qualified." Most of us do not need a crystal ball to tell us how many Negro Americans the Birch Society would find to be "qualified."

As far as Negro voting rights are concerned, the John Birch Society is much more than a kissing cousin of the State of Mississippi, where only 3.89 percent of the Negro citizens of voting age are permitted to register, with an even smaller percentage permitted to vote.

The Birch Society can claim Mississippi kinship, also, on the Supreme Court and segregation issue for Mississippi's Senator James O. Eastland told a Senatobia, Miss., crowd in 1955 that It was "obligated to defy" the ruling of the Court.

In addition to this, there is the hard-core resistance as evidenced in more than 250 laws and ordinances passed by panic-stricken Southern State legislatures and distraught city councils to avert the fulfillment of the Supreme Court's order to desegregate the public school system "with all deliberate speed!"

TELLING A NEGLECTED STORY

To say that such laws and ordinances are unconstitutional is putting it mildly. They are little short of subversive. These anti-freedom legislators have forgotten that it is still written in the Constitution that "no state shall make or enforce any law which shall abridge the privileges or immunities of the citizens of the United States...."

Since the student sit-in demonstrations spread across the country, more than 150 trespass and disorderly conduct laws have been hastily passed by perplexed state and city legislators to permit the arrest of non-violent, hymn-singing, Bible-reading demonstrators and picketers, who have dramatized the withholding of basic equal rights from all Americans. These laws, passed in the fever-heat of anger and of adhesion to a social concept stemming from the dark ages have been proved unconstitutional and they are also ungodly!

I do not have to remind this delegation from the Branches of our great organization that these recent repressive acts against student sit-ins and Freedom Riders are not the first of their kind. We of the NAACP know what repression means. Louisiana, Texas, Florida, Georgia, Arkansas, Mississippi, Virginia, South Carolina and Alabama have taken various steps against either our organization or our members.

They have enacted special laws. They have set up legislative investigating committees. They have used the Communist smear. They have tried in every way to get our membership list. Father Theodore Gibson, the courageous president of our Miami, Fla., Branch, faces a $1,200 fine and six months in jail because he has refused to reveal the names of NAACP members to a legislative committee.

As a result of the actions of the states and of the inflammatory public statements of some state officials and legislators, too many of our people have lost their jobs and their credit. Some of their homes have been bombed and shot into. NAACP state and local leaders and their families have been threatened. Violence has been used.

Despite all this, we <u>have beaten them off</u>. Wherever we have had a chance to fight even on the ground they themselves have chosen, we have defeated them. The Louisiana and Arkansas laws have been struck down. The Virginia laws are still in court. The Florida thing is still on appeal. Only Alabama remains as it was on June 1, 1956, and that is because the Alabama courts thus far have refused to place our case on the docket for a hearing, after the state was reversed by the U. S. Supreme Court.

Not only have our lawyers won in the courts, but our people in the communities have won in spiritual battles.

The NAACP is operating in Mississippi and in every Southern state, except Alabama. Our local units are active In those states. We have there a <u>moving</u>, not a <u>holding</u> organization. I could call the roll tonight from El Paso, Texas, to Alexandria, Virginia, and throughout that sweep across our Southland, NAACP voices, confident and unafraid, would answer with the deeds they have done under the strafing of the enemy. The best proof of this courageous pushing power - not mere survival power - is to be found in the fact that for last year, that is, for 1960, the NAACP had a gain of 46,412 in membership.

So, everything they have been able to throw against the recent demonstrations and the steady and victorious hammering of the NAACP has not stopped the drive toward freedom.

Tonight, your Board Chairman calls for a <u>phalanx</u> of <u>freedom fighters</u> that will win the war, not just battles. We have shed too many tears of both despair and joy, we have sacrificed too much blood of too many pioneers and martyrs to be carried away in this late day by the euphony of a new slogan, or by the symphonic repetition of old and enduring truisms. The founders of the two pure Negro Methodisms in America rose from their knees in segregated church balconies in 1789 and 1796, respectively and declared that segregation must go.

We are too old in the ways of the long struggle that has engaged our fathers and forefathers not to realize that wars are won by using every available military resource and not by the employment of raiding parties alone.

The dramatic exposure of segregation practices and of law enforcement procedures Is useful in awakening a complacent public opinion among white and colored Americans, but to suggest that Its function in the Great War goes much beyond this is to confuse a signal flare with a barrage.

In calling for a phalanx of fighters, we Invite all to join in the drive to a victory. That has been made sure by the varied and brilliant tactics and the steady pounding of our NAACP.

It was the NAACP legal victory that planted the immovable stone on the grave of bus segregation in Montgomery, Alabama. Although the sit-in technique had been used against single stores, it was NAACP young people who pioneered its use in 1958 against whole communities in Kansas, Oklahoma and Missouri.

We have banished the Jim Crow railroad car and the Jim Crow bus and air terminals are on their way out. A Negro woman of Brooklyn, N.Y., who was dragged from her Pullman berth in Florida in 1927 and for whom NAACP attorneys won a law suit and damages was one of those who went crying into the wilderness ahead of today's Freedom Riders.

We have led the American people through the deserts represented by the Elaine, Arl., riot and persecution, by the famous Sweet case in Detroit, and by the long blood bath of lynching. Where there were no roads through these wastelands of proscription and hatred, we built them. Where there were no precedents, we set them. Where there had been no hope, we fashioned it. Where there was either no law or a perversion thereof, we built new law. Where there were no guideposts, we planted them for those who were to follow. Where public opinion was indifferent or hostile, we drove home truth and aroused concern.

We have led the people across the mountains in a trek that outlawed the White Primary, struck down the restrictive real estate covenants and brought forth the epoch-making Supreme Court school decisions of 1938 through 1954.

And, by God's help, we will lead all Americans into the <u>green-pastures</u> of equal rights under the Constitution and to the <u>still waters</u> of the democracy encroached in the American dream.

Tonight we call upon the traffic tower - the White House - to clear the runways for the final take-off to freedom. We appreciate the brave words of the Kennedys, the President and the Attorney General, regarding civil rights. Our President has made it unmistakably clear that this area is a matter of personal as well as political concern to him. The Attorney General has moved vigorously to enforce constitutional rights, particularly in voting and public accommodations. In a score of ways he has emphasized the President's attitude.

Officially, he has issued instructions and directives to his department heads. He and Vice President Lyndon B. Johnson see-eye to eye on the function of the President's Committee on Equal Job Opportunity. Moreover, he has made some unusual appointments to office, one of which we have hailed with great satisfaction, although our Government's gain in Dr. Robert C. Weaver was our loss in the NAACP. All Americans, white and black, and all cities will get a better deal In housing because of the heart and head of that superior public servant, Bob Weaver.

Our Attorney General went down into Georgia and made an unprecedented speech on what the Department of Justice will do in protecting constitutional rights. Only four days ago the Attorney General made known the Department's action in the State of Mississippi against practices which violate the 1957 and 1960 voter registration laws.

A picture of Robert Kennedy's role in the Alabama bus riots is furnished by Gov. Patterson's charge that the young Attorney General "ordered him around." We don't know whether it is true or not, but if it seemed that way to Gov. Patterson, then Robert Kennedy is a rare Attorney General, indeed. He can make mistakes. In fact, he already has slipped up with his "cooling off" advice, but anyone who gives the likes of Patterson a hot foot is entitled to a few slips.

But with all this, there is missing from the picture of the first half-year of this Administration any move to enact the legislation so necessary to back up the pronouncements and actions of the Executive Branch of government. To repeat a cliché, ours is a government of laws, not of men. It

is to the enduring law that the citizen must look for protection of his rights and for redress of his grievances, not to passing personalities, no matter how upright or courageous.

Too many minds, especially those in legislative halls and in political organizations, are not clear in their concepts of democracy. We must summon every resource and exert every pressure to convert the American mind to the pressing importance of full freedom for every citizen.

This full freedom, as every schoolboy now knows, means the abolition of differential treatment based upon race and religion in every area of American life: education, voting and government, employment, housing, travel, recreation and general public accommodation. We can thus be an inspiration and a guide to the new nations of Asia, Africa and the Caribbean instead of a bitter reproach.

We must make clear to our fellow citizens that the fullness of this individual freedom is important to the United States in this crisis struggle between Communism and the West. Let us make no mistake. We must make democracy real and workable for every American, not specifically to make a good impression on any nation or to win any people "to our side." We must do this because it is right and, in righteous practicality, because only in this way can we build an indomitable inner national spirit that will enable us to define and to enrich the free life.

Now is the time for us in the NAACP to <u>capitalize our gains</u>. Every Branch has the history of 52 years of a solid, relentless, successful, tireless fight-for-freedom as the justifiable and proud basis for appeals for memberships and redoubled support. Life memberships are at an all-time high; the Fighting Fund for Freedom has been administered to great advantage; we have supported those upon whom reprisals have been visited because of their fight for freedom; we have aligned ourselves with, and given moral and financial support to, every worthwhile effort toward civil rights and every non-subversive organization essaying to enter this field. Our May 25 directive to Branch officers spelled out our support of the Freedom Rides.

The brave children who went through Little Rock, Clinton and New Orleans; the fearless youth who marched through showers of stones, brickbats and fire hosing, who walked the gauntlet of baseball bats, drawn police guns and the canine corps, who went to jail and returned to their non-violent demonstrations to be jailed again -all these compose a mighty army, produced by a half century of our Association's indoctrination and victorious activities.

They and the adults who backed them up constitute the inspiring fruit of our NAACP struggle, ready to carry on until freedom is won. We here tonight, therefore, should be re-inspired and re-dedicated to serve in the ranks of the freedom fighters through the National Association for the Advancement of Colored People.

After a dissertation upon those who had kept the faith, the author of the book, Hebrews, sums up the situation with these spectacular words: (Hebrews 12:1)

"Wherefore seeing we also are compassed about with so great a cloud of witnesses...."

Tonight I am sure we are surrounded not only by the present-day witnesses across the land, but by the men and women who founded the National Association for the Advancement of Colored People and those who have carried our banners and sat in the tents of our strategy: Oswald Garrison Villard, Jane Addams, Ida B. Wells Barnett, Mary White Ovington, Stephen B. Wise, Alexander Walters, J. Milton Waldron, William English Walling, Nannie Burroughs, W.E.B. DuBois, Joel E. Spingarn, Florence Kelly, Moorfield Storey, James Weldon Johnson, William Pickens, Walter White and an innumerable host!

They tell us to carry on. From their vantage point, they can see the world ahead; they know our cause will not fail; they see democracy across the nation and around the world as a prelude to earth's redemption for the Kingdom of God.

Let us tighten our seat belts and adjust our space suit for <u>the final thrust to freedom</u>. Surely, in the world ahead, will come the day when traffic will be cleared and from the legislative, judicial and executive branches of our government will come the count-down for the Stage Three rocket trip to freedom.

Segregation's walls will fall. Discrimination's towers will tumble. And Americans, those stemming from the original Indians; the Nordics, Slavs and Latins from Europe; our fathers, the survivors of the infamous African slave trade, and those whose immigrant parents were of yellow, brown and mixed bloods -all will enter a new realm of true democracy, under our Constitution, under the Stars and Stripes, under God!

APPENDIX SEVEN

BUILDING AND USING THE POWER OF THE GHETTO
By
Bishop Stephen Gill Spottswood

Fifty nine years ago the founders of the National Association for the Advancement of Colored People adopted a series of goals with the avowed purpose to make the Negro American: Physically free from lynching, Socially free from segregation, Educationally free from ignorance, Politically free from disenfranchisement, Economically free from employment discrimination, Residentially free from housing restrictions.

We have not receded one inch from these goals and, having developed the largest, most effective, most successful Civil Rights organization in the world, we continue on our chosen path of education, negotiation, political action, court decisions, legislation and non-violent direct action to make the dreams of the fathers come true.

Major victories have been achieved in every field mentioned in the original goals and the steady march of our hosts, a half-millionstrong, has brought complete and lasting victory within the foresight of all of us here tonight.

THE RISE OF THE GHETTO

The city in human history is the saga of mankind. From the beginnings of civilization to this final third of the twentieth century men have trended toward the city. The pattern of housing segregation has created black ghettos in almost all United States cities.

Dr. Kenneth B. Clarke, in his "Dark Ghetto" says, "The dark ghetto's invisible walls have been erected by the white society, by those who have power, both to confine those who have no power and to perpetuate their powerlessness. The dark ghettos are social, political, educational, and - above all - economic colonies. Their inhabitants are subject peoples, victims of the greed, cruelty, insensibility, guilt and fear their masters. The ghetto is ferment, paradox, conflict, and dilemma. Yet, within its pervasive pathology exists, a surprising human resilience."

THE PLIGHT OF THE GHETTO

There is no more pathetic picture of inner-city blight than that of the American black ghetto. Old (100 years in many instances) houses in hopeless need of repair. Streets sagging and humped and littered. An average of forty human beings lodged in five and six rooms. Broken plumbing and broken windows and broken homes are a patent combination. Here live the people of the highest unemployment rate and with the lowest incomes, in many instances far below subsistence level. Its whole gamut is rats, absentee, feudal-like landlords, loan sharks, exploiting merchants and services, canine-corps police, inadequate schools ad infinitum, ad nauseam. From this we have the plight of the ghetto millions; poverty, frustration and despair!

The plight of the ghetto is the background of the riots. While we do not condone looting, burning and sniping, whether perpetrated by black or white ghetto residents or by policemen, National guardsmen or Federal troops, we mind America that for 59 years the NAACP has been striving to remove the strangling inequalities of the ghetto which have stimulated the riots. We have every sympathy for the people of despair who have revolted in hundreds of our cities.

The N.A.A.C.P. is involved in the plight of the ghettos. Most of our Branch leaders live on the ghettos. A vast majority of our urban Branch offices are in the ghetto. We are engaged in counsel and guidance for acceptable welfare. We have demanded the repeal of the welfare section of the Social Security bill because it is inadequate and unrealistic provisions.

Our dynamic Branch program led by the prince of Directors, Gloster B. Current, calls for the organization of Negro contractors, so that they will be big enough to compete with larger contractors and bring a larger payroll to the ghetto. Branches are developing files of Negro contractors and making referrals to potential customers who were unaware of the availability of those small business men.

The oft-used and frequently misused phrase, "black power1' has been the motto of the Association's economic program for fifty years.

Black power lies in the realm of the Negro's economic advancement. We raise the question--How much money into the black banks, the black building and loan associations, the black cooperative funds, the black grocery stores and variety stores by those of us who advocate black power? Our Branches are called upon to use their power to the funding of Negro business. We must sponsor corporations in the retail mercantile establishment. Every Branch should have an Economic Development Committee. There should be Branch leadership representation of the entire community. Branches must say, to the ghetto landlord, for instance, "Spend your rehabilitation money here, where you collect your money!"

To build black power, we must have in increase in skilled people: Negro physicians, dentists, lawyers, teachers, clergymen, engineers, mathematicians and scientists. We must utilize available scholarships and educational funding.

Here, let me pay tribute to the indefatigable leadership of Roy Wilkins on the National Advisory Commission on Civil Disorders. Had it not been for the effective role played by our Executive Director in the formation of the Commission's report, the direct action recommended would be devoid of practical value. Patiently, tirelessly he insisted that direct, positive action by the government and the people of the United States would be the only way to avoid civil disorders and "save the peace of the nation."

Let us give full credit to President Johnson in the battle for full freedom for all Americans. Beside the appointing of commissions to study the social ills of the country, more Civil Rights legislation has been proposed and enacted in the Lyndon Baines Johnson administration than under all other presidents combined. He has personally espoused Civil Rights legislation plus general welfare, education and anti-poverty programs.

The N.A.A.C.P. pledges to cooperate, participate and lead on the fulfillment of the recommendations of the report of the National Advisory Commission; thru its 1800 odd Branches, Youth Councils, College Chapters, State Conferences, Regional Conferences and National Convention.

We are involved! We must do all in our power to prevent riots. We must speedily bring about the total fulfillment of the Association1 goals. We are soul-brothers in the plight of the ghetto!

We are for the strengthening of the ghetto but not for the development of the ghetto-state. The true definition of an American ghetto is a designated area from which you cannot get out. The black ghettos of the United States must be eliminated by our entrance to and participation in all the benefits of our country. Hence, our task is to create housing and employment in suburbia as well as within the inner-city.

TELLING A NEGLECTED STORY
THE POWER OF THE GHETTO

There is number of Negro Americans in almost every major industry in our country. unlimited potential in the ghetto. Talent without restriction, fabulous intelligence and great, productive proclivity lie dormant within a thousand inner cities of our country.

As an Association, we are geared to build and use the power of the ghetto. Our Department of Labor and Industry, led by an intrepid director, Herbert Hill, has worked unceasingly for black economic power. In a large measure, we are responsible for the current break-thru in good jobs and upgrading enjoyed by an increasing number of Negro Americans in almost every major industry in our country.

In this, the centennial year of William Edward Burkhardt DuBois, we are following the DuBois formula for black power: political power! First of all, our Washington Bureau, thru the brilliant leadership of Clarence Mitchell, has become the most powerful, most respected, most consulted lobby on Capitol Hill.

The N.A.A.C.P. is the pioneer in voter registration and voter education. We have never forgotten our role in developing black political power. An example is the 150,000 voters brought back to rolls in South Carolina last year and our goal in the Palmetto for 1968 is 250,000 voters. We have been at this business since 1915. Who amassed the political power that sent Oscar DePriest to the Congress forty years ago? and Dr. Singleton to Nebraska's unicameral Legislature in 1928? The N.A.A.C.P.!

There is unlimited potential in the "heart" of our cities. Who can predict the force of those millions when their sheer numbers are organized and directed? The Kinetics needed to round out this century, not as a century of segregation, riots and martyrs like George Lee, Medgar Evers, Goodman, Schwerner and Chaney, Vernon Dahmer Wharlest Jackson, Johnathan Reeb, Viola Liuzzo, the Kennedys and Martin Luther King, but a century of freedom are locked up in the ghettos, awaiting our leadership.

Here, let me pay tribute to Doctor King, the most eloquent speaker for human rights in our time. His voice was heard around the world. His "call to preach" found fulfillment in his indefatigable labors on behalf of freedom, peace and anti-poverty. Like his predecessor in the church, St. Paul, he was "beaten with many stripes"--exposed continually to false-arrest and sent to jail. He was harried police dogs. His home was bombed. His daily life was a risk--a calculated risk of his uncompromising position and intrepid pursuit of his goals. Dedication to freedom was his watch-word and love for mankind, his motto. When the history of this century is written, his name will be inscribed in gold and his message embellished with silver!

POOR PEOPLE'S MARCH

The power of the ghetto is focused in the proposals of the poor people's march:

Every employable citizen has the right to a meaningful job at decent wage. The Poor are not lazy. In fact the vast majority toil hours at menial, underpaid labor. Their wages must be raised. New careers must be created for them—in building decent housing for all; in raising the level of education, health and social care: in reconstructing and beautifying America. This is not makework. This is meaningful work that goes to the heart of our nation's needs.

Every citizen who cannot work be guaranteed an adequate income as a matter of right. A thousand economics of varying persuasions have called for a guaranteed annual income as morally necessary and economically sound.

We recognize that this economic bill of rights cannot be adopted overnight And we are not blind to the conservative mood of the present Congress. But we shall not
sit back and let the forces of reaction and cynicism win the day. This nation can and must take specific, tangible steps toward redeeming the American promise. We shall therefore make the following immediate demands:

I We call upon the President and all Presidential candidates to endorse the basic principles of an economic bill of rights.

II We demand that Congress, in his session,

1. Recommit the Federal Government to the Full Eminent Act of 1946 and a creation of at least one million socially useful career jobs in public service.

2. Adopt the pending housing and urban development act of 1963.

3. Repeal the 90th Congress's punitive welfare restrictions, which put a freeze on the number of families eligible for welfare aid, compel mothers of preschool children to seek employment and deny assistance in unemployed fathers unless they can produce evidence of previous employment.

4. Extend to all farm workers the right—guaranteed under

the National Labor Relations Acts-to organize and bargain collectively.

5. Restore budget cuts for bilingual education. Head Start, summer jobs, Economic Opportunity Act, Elementary and Secondary Education Act.

III We further call upon the President to declare a national emergency and, under his present statutory authority:

1. Institute food distribution programs wherever severe hunger exists in America.
2. Provide free food stamps to those who cannot afford to buy them.
3. Help poor farmers set up cooperatives.
4. End discrimination in the food offices of the Agriculture Department.
5. Give the poor first priority in existing health programs and create health services in isolated rural areas.
6. Include the poor in the planning and administration of Federal programs at local levels.

APPENDIX EIGHT

Burning Hearts

Stephen Gill Spottswood

Luke 24:32—*"Did not our heart burn within us while He talked to us by the way?"*

 We are debtors to Luke for the New Testament details of the most human post-resurrection dramas. The events of the first Easter afternoon and evening recorded by the physician-biographer of Jesus Christ constitute magnificent treatment of life-situations in the experience of first century men and we easily see their counterparts in the drama of our own period.

 The setting was the road from Jerusalem to Emmaus, a winding path: seven and a half miles long that found its way through shaded hills and barren stretches that afforded the vivid contrasts of a beautiful eastern Springtime and rocky wastes, suggesting the dialectic of life and human experience. The time was "toward evening"—approaching the twilight hour that has always engaged the spirit of man in contemplation.

> "I love to steal awhile away
>
> From every cumbering care,
>
> And spend the hours of setting day
>
> In humble, grateful prayer"

 It is not hard to imagine the colorful countryside along the Emmaus road decked in the deep gold and orange shades of setting sun and the accompanying silhouettes reflected and refracted by the clouds in rich browns and rock purples and brasses. The cast of characters was drawn from widespread sources. Cleopas (renowned father) and his companion were walking down the road as the curtain of events was lifted. When their dialog ended and they reached the bed-rock of reasoning, Jesus appeared in the second scene unrecognized, and entered the conversation and so inspired the travelers that they wanted Him to be their guest. He withdrew and the final scene was enacted in Jerusalem where "the eleven" remaining disciples were gathered in fellowship, rejoicing together that their Lord had risen "as He said."

TELLING A NEGLECTED STORY

The Story

The story abounds in psychological suggestions for the experience of the men on the road to Emmaus twenty centuries ago and for men today who will journey together in the quest for peace of mind and the salvation of the human race. The narrative declares "they talked together." They did not pursue their journey in silence, brooding over the events of the Passover-week-end in Jerusalem. They talked through the situation covered by the first Holy Week. There is value in talking. The sound of the human voice—the exchange of ideas and the play of one personality upon another in conversation combine to make men sense the value of companionship and reteaches the fact that "all men are brothers". When one discovers that the interest in a topic of conversation is mutual, respect for the other's personality heightens and equalitarian awareness is mutually appreciated. The next step in the Emmaus drama is described in the rich clause, "They communed together"; redundant rhetoric but undoubtedly employed to emphasize the oneness of their thought and the mutual experience they enjoyed. When men talk "the same language" (and for this stage of development of one-world, shall we say, 'use language that has the same meaning in human experience' they are apt to find themselves in communion. The similarities of human experience definitely outnumber the differences that lie between men. Jacques Maritain, modern French philosopher stresses this thought in the area of religion when he raises the question: "How should we all be called upon to love one another in God if we were not all equal in our condition and specific dignity as rational creatures?" He answers in part when he exhorts: "Each of us should faithyfully witness, according as his state of life permits, the love of God for all beings and the respect due to the image of God in each human creature."

Finally the Emmaus travelers graduated to the plane of reasoning: "They talked together—they communed together and they *reasoned*." What conclusions of faith they developed and the tenor of their logic are obscured by the sudden entrance of Jesus. Luke succinctly puts the master on the scene with the word, "Jesus himself drew near!" As in Galilee, He introduced himself by asking questions: "What manner of communications are these that ye have one to another, as ye walk, and are sad?" Then Cleopas poured out the story of the Holy Week. What relief there must have been for him to tell how the Master of men had suffered and died! But his story included the events of that morning at the sepulcher. When he had finished, the Third Traveller [sic] cried, "O fools and slow of heart to believe—ought not Christ to have suffered these things and to have entered into his glory?"

The obvious lesson here for us today—those who doubt the power of God for human salvation—those who question the Ethics of Jesus for world economy—those who prefer to merely worship Christ rather than to follow him in the emulation of service—is that when we talk together—commune together and reason, Christ comes into our midst, gives us leadership, exhorts us to full

157

faith and constrains us to live like him despite the deterrants [sic] of our civilization to Christian living. As through a mist, the men on the Emmaus road experience, as Jesus talked to them, a sentiment expressed by Thomas Curtis Clark who sings,

> "There was a man—or was he but a man?—
>
> Who walked alone with God… at his side
>
> Walked other men, they could not know his dreams;
>
> They scorned his lofty words. His eye could scan
>
> The secrets of the stars and lo! They cried,
>
> "This man is mad!" But, blinded by the gleams
>
> Of dawning glory, still he loved and sang,
>
> He sang of beauty, sang of faith and hope,
>
> And little children gladly heard his songs,
>
> But men—tho' all the bells of heaven rang
>
> With joy of him—they could but blindly grope.
>
> They railed upon him, took brute whips with thongs,
>
> And foully beat him. Him at last they slew,
>
> Who, dying, cried: "They know not what they do!"

Three Great Experiences

Three great experiences came out of the intercourse of the travelers on the road to Emmaus. As they approached the village and sensed the departure of Jesus, they uttered the famous intreaty: "Abide with us—for it is toward evening and the day is far spent." This preacher yearns for men to give the master of men such an invitation. We need to invite Jesus to our twentieth century homes. Were He our Guest, the whole level of living would be lifted to the higher plane that God has decreed the goal of human experience. Were Christ abiding in our homes, there would be no difficulty in keeping the Ten Commandments and following the Golden Rule. His spirit would penetrate every area of our civilization. The problems of human economy would be solved and the world would be united for abundant living and creative thinking and spiritual appreciation.

In the familiar role of Guest-Host in Cleopas' house, as He broke and distributed the bread of their simple meal, the second great experience occurred. "Their eyes were opened, and they knew him". O that men were possessed today of such a sight—that they might see the living Christ against the background of a trouble world: the Christ of peace in a war-mad century; the Christ of unifying brotherhood in a world of nationalism competing for empires and balances of power; the Christ of the Mount in a world that seeks for laws continued within limitations of a history punctuated by the failure of any code short of the Jesus standard of truth and love.

Then he faded out of the room an in the exultancy of purged souls they cried, "Did not our heart burn within us, while He talked with us by the way?" Heart warming experience is always the final blessing of fellowship with Jesus Christ. In Him was God's (quod erat demonstrandum_ *what was to be proved*: The truth of the eternal God was to live in men and pentrate [sic] their relationships until in the unity of BURNING HEARTS, they would redeem the world and bring the fabulous Kingdom of God to the earth.

Burning Hearts Today

We need *burning hearts* today to talk together concerning the problems of peace, security, race and unity. George Buttrick, in his provocative book, "Christ and Man's Dilemma" says, "Christ is redemption from all our ignorance—we could not foresee the Negro problem, but men would never have trafficked in slaves if they had taken Christ as truth. We could not guess that the machine would make congestion, slums and ominous unrest: but we could never have herded adults to say nothing of children, into old-time factories if we had taken Christ as truth. We could not know that the Exclusion Act and the sale of armaments to Japan would help to bring a devastating war, but we would never have been party to such policies if we had taken Christ at truth—when He is our Truth—instead of walking in the shadows of man's wisdom', we walk in the light that rules the changing years."

We need *burning hearts* for the communion demanded by the challenge of this high hour of the world's history. The wrecks of the past urge the United Nations, world economy, the brotherhood of man—the oneness of the world. There is logic in Christ's way of life—there is logic in a united world. History, science and religion all agree that the three great experiences on the road to Emmaus are needed—first in the heart of the individual and spreading until they occur in the hearts of the nations. Hearts warmed by the fires of religion—in the fellowship of Christ become the crusading, *Burning Hearts* who find others who can say, 'The Lord is risen indeed' and go forth to save the world in truth for abundant living and the Kingdom of God.

Goethe's Easter Chorus from Faust expresses the passion of Burning Hearts:

> "Christ is arisen!
>
> Joy to the mortal One,
>
> Whom the unmerited
>
> Needs did imprison.
>
> Christ is ascended!
>
> Bliss hath invested him—
>
> Woes that molested him,
>
> Trials that tested him,
>
> Gloriously ended!
>
> Christ is arisen
>
> Out of corruption's womb
>
> Burst ye the prison,
>
> Break from your gloom!
>
> Praising and pleading him,
>
> Lovingly needing him
>
> Brotherly feeding him,
>
> Preaching and speeding him,
>
> Blessing, succeeding Him,
>
> Thus is the master near,--
>
> Thus is He here!

TELLING A NEGLECTED STORY

APPENDIX NINE

"Take Another Look"

"And Elijah said to his servant, go up, now, look towards the sea; And he went up, and looked, and said, there is nothing. And, Elijah said, go again, and look a second time."

1 kings 18:44

BISHOP SHAW'S LAST ANNUAL CONFERENCE SERMON
AS DELIVERED IN THE YEAR OF OUR LORD, 1979

"COME HOLY SPIRIT, HEAVENLY DOVE, WITH ALL THY QUICKENING POWERS;
KINDLE A FLAME OF SACRED LOVE IN THESE COLD HEARTS OF OURS.
"IN VAIN WE TUNE OUR FORMAL SONGS, IN VAIN WE STRIVE TO RISE;
HOSANNAS LANGUISH ON OUR TONGUES, AND OUR DEVOTION DIES."
LOOK HOW WE GROVEL HERE BELOW, FOND OF THESE EARTHLY TOILS - LOOK UPON US - WE WANT YOU TO KNOW THAT WE'RE HERE. WE'RE WEAK. WE'RE WEARY AND WE'RE WORN. HELP US DEAR MASTER. IN THY NAME WE PRAY. AMEN.

I SPEAK TO MY BROTHERS, IN CHAINS - SPIRITUAL CHAINS. ELIJAH, TO ME, HAS ALWAYS BEEN AN INTERESTING PROPHET. HE'S THE FIRST LUMINARY THAT COMES OUT UPON THE PROPHETIC STAGE. FIRST, AFTER THE JUDGES, WE SEE ELIJAH STEP OUT. MOSES STEPPED OUT WITH HIS LAW, ABRAHAM STEPPED OUT WITH HIS FAITH, AND THEN CAME THE JUDGES - OF WHOM, PERHAPS, SAMUEL HAS WRITTEN. AND, AFTER SAMUEL, GOD SENT HIS PROPHETS.

NOW, WE WILL NOTICE THAT GOD'S PROPHETS, WHO WERE DETERMINED TO DO WHAT GOD BADE THEM DO; TOLD THEM TO DO; AND, OFTEN AT A DIFFICULT TIME - MEN WOULD NOT RECEIVE THEM. HE SENT SOME TO DESTROY. MEN SOUGHT TO GET RID OF THEM, BUT, ELIJAH - THE TISHBITE - GOD'S PROPHET, SPOKE IN A WAY THAT MADE MEN KNOW THAT HE WAS UNAFRAID, BECAUSE HE SPOKE FOR GOD. AND, LET US REMEMBER, THAT WHEN GOD'S PROPHET SPEAKS HE DOESN'T SPEAK FOR HIMSELF. GOD'S PROPHET CANNOT SPEAK IN HIS OWN NAME. FOR, ONCE HE BEGINS TO SPEAK IN HIS OWN NAME, HE CEASES TO BE A PROPHET. HE CEASES TO HAVE A PROPHETIC MESSAGE. ELIJAH WAS UNAFRAID, BECAUSE HE REPRESENTED GOD. MOST OF US WHEN WE START OUT, YOU KNOW, AND EVERYTHING IS GOING WELL WITH US, AND EVERYONE IS TELLING YOU HOW GOOD IT IS THAT YOU'VE DECIDED TO COME OUT ON GOD'S SIDE - YOU THINK THAT IT'S ALL GOING TO BE A BED OF ROSES. BUT, DOWN THE LINE YOU'LL FIND OUT, THAT THERE ARE OPPOSITIONS SOMETIMES.

GOD HAD SENT ELIJAH TO KING AHAB, WHILE HE WAS ON THE THRONE. AND, YOU KNOW, OF COURSE, THAT AHAB HAD MARRIED JEZEBEL - AND JEZEBEL WAS A VERY STRONGMINDED WOMAN.

161

SHE SEEMED TO HAVE HAD SOME CONTROL OVER AHAB. I HOPE WE PREACHERS HAVE NO JEZEBELS WHO HAVE CONTROL OVER US - WITH APOLOGIES TO THE GOOD WIVES. NEVERTHELESS, BAD ADVISE CAN COME TO YOU FROM PEOPLE VERY CLOSE TO YOU. AHAB AND JEZEBEL HATED ELIJAH. THE ONLY REASON THEY HATED ELIJAH, WAS BECAUSE ELIJAH WAS GOD'S PROPHET. MANY TIMES WE ARE HATED, NOT BECAUSE OF OURSELVES - BUT, BECAUSE OF WHOM WE REPRESENT. AND, WHEN YOU REPRESENT - AND TRULY REPRESENT, THE ONE THAT SENT YOU, YOU CAN'T COMPROMISE. YOU CAN'T NEGOTIATE. YOU CAN'T STRADDLE THE FENCE. YOU'VE GOT TO SAY, "THUS SAITH THE LORD." TAKE IT, OR LEAVE IT.

JEZEBEL AND AHAB WANTED ELIJAH TO CHANGE HIS MODE - HIS FORMAT. ELIJAH, ON ONE OCCASION, WHEN HE WAS COMING TO MEET AHAB, SAID TO OBADIAH: "OBADIAH, I WANT YOU TO GO AND TELL AHAB THAT ELIJAH IS HERE. TELL HIM - TELL HIM, ELIJAH IS HERE." OBADIAH WAS AFRAID. HE SAID TO ELIJAH: "AHAB HAS BEEN TRYING TO PUT YOU OUT OF BUSINESS FOR A LONG TIME. HE'S GOT HIS ARMIES - HIS MEN OUT, SEARCHING FOR YOU. AND, IF THEY FIND YOU, THEY'RE GOING TO SLAY YOU. AND, IF I GO AND TELL HIM THAT YOU'RE HERE AND HE SENDS HIS SOLDIER HERE, AND YOU'RE NOT HERE - HE'S GOING TO KILL ME." THE OLD MAN SAID: "OBADIAH, GO AND TELL AHAB THAT ELIJAH IS HERE. NO MATTER WHOM HE SENDS, I'LL BE HERE WHEN THEY GET HERE. NOT ONLY WILL I BE HERE, BUT, GOD WILL BE HERE ALSO, RIGHT BY MY SIDE."

GOD'S PROPHETS MUST LEARN TO TRUST IN GOD. NO MATTER WHAT BETIDES. NO MATTER WHAT HAPPENS. YOU MUST STAND IN THE FAITH, ONCE DELIVERED UNTO THE SAINTS. IF YOU DO ANY LESS, YOU'LL BE A TRAITOR, AS TO THE CAUSE. IF YOU DO ANY LESS, YOU'LL BE UNWORTHY OF THE BLESSING AND THE HERESY.

OBADIAH DELIVERED THE MESSAGE, CALMLY. THEN, AHAB CAME DOWN TO ELIJAH AND SAID: "WHAT'S THE TROUBLE HERE? WHAT'S GOING ON HERE?" ELIJAH SAID: "WELL, I'LL TELL YOU WHAT'S GOING ON - YOU AND JEZEBEL WONT DO RIGHT. YOU'RE THE KING ALRIGHT, BUT REMEMBER, YOU'RE THE KING DOWN HERE. YOU'VE GOT TO REMEMBER, THAT THERE'S A KING UP THERE. AND, THE KING UP THERE HAS DECLARED, THAT YOU AND JEZEBEL ARE NOT RIGHT. YOU'RE NOT LIVING RIGHT. YOU'RE NOT LEADING THE PEOPLE RIGHT. YOU'RE NOT DOING RIGHT - NOT CARRYING OUT GOD'S BIDDINGS. AND, FOR THAT REASON GOD SENT ME TO TELL YOU, THAT, IT AIN'T - GONNA RAIN - NO MORE." HE MIGHT NOT HAVE SAID IT THAT WAY, BUT, THAT'S WHAT IT MEANT. GOD IS GOING TO LOCK UP THE HEAVENS - AND, HE'S GOING TO KEEP THEM LOCKED UP, UNTIL YOU'VE CHANGED YOUR MIND.

YOU KNOW, NO MATTER HOW MUCH YOU ARE AGAINST GOD'S PROPHET - NO MATTER HOW MANY THINGS YOU DO AGAINST HIM, GOD'S GOT A WAY OF OVERCOMING THE OPPOSITIONS. I SAID, GOD'S GOT A WAY OF OVERCOMING THE OPPOSITIONS.

THE HEAVENS WERE SHUT UP FOR THREE YEARS. OLD MAN AHAB GOT WORRIED WHEN ALL THE CATTLE WERE DYING - THE CHILDREN WERE DYING - THE PEOPLE WERE STARVING, ALL THE GRASS AND GRAIN WAS GONE. HE WAS IN TROUBLE. AND, YOU KNOW, THEY MAY NOT LIKE GOD'S PROPHETS - THEY MAY NOT ADMIRE GOD'S PROPHETS - THEY MAY NOT LOVE GOD'S PROPHETS. BUT, ONE THING - WHENEVER THEY GET IN TROUBLE, THEY TURN TO GOD'S PROPHETS. YOU DONT HEAR ME THIS MORNING - YOU DONT EVEN KNOW I'M PREACHING HERE! WHENEVER THEY GET IN TROUBLE, THEY KNOW WHERE GOD'S MAN IS. IF THEY'VE BEEN TALKING ABOUT HIM - THEY STOP TALKING ABOUT HIM. IF THEY'VE BEEN LIEING ON HIM, THEY STOP LIEING ON HIM. HE USE TO BE A BAD MAN, BUT, NOW HE'S A GOOD MAN. HE'S A GOOD MAN NOW, BECAUSE THEY NEED HIM. HALLELUJAH - I NEED HIM NOW.

WELL, ELIJAH SAID: "AS LONG AS YOU FEEL LIKE THAT, WHY DONT YOU CALL ON JEZEBEL'S GOD? HE MIGHT CAN DO SOMETHING ABOUT THIS FAMINE." OBADIAH SAID: THEY CAN'T DO NOTHING ABOUT THIS FAMINE - WE'VE BEEN CALLING ON HIM, A LONG TIME." ELIJAH SAID: "WELL, I'LL SEE WHAT I CAN DO ABOUT IT. YOU GO ON BACK UP TO YOUR PALACE AND LEAVE IT TO ME." HALLELUJAH! IT'S A GOOD THING WHEN YOU CAN SAY TO YOUR PEOPLE, "GO ON NOW - GO BACK HOME. I'LL TAKE YOUR CASE UP WITH THE KING. I'LL TALK TO GOD ABOUT

TELLING A NEGLECTED STORY

YOUR TROUBLES. YOU STAY THERE - UNTIL I TELL YOU WHAT GOD HAS TO TELL YOU." YOU HAVE TO BE A MAN OF GOD. YOU HAVE TO KNOW GOD. I DONT MEAN KNOW ABOUT GOD! BUT, KNOWING GOD FOR YOURSELF - SO MUCH, SO THAT YOU CAN DEPEND ON HIM. ELIJAH SAID: "GO OUT THERE NOW, AND LOOK. TAKE A LOOK. LOOK TOWARD THE SEA." SO MANY OF US LOOK - BUT, WE DONT KNOW WHERE TO LOOK. WE DONT KNOW HOW TO LOOK. WE DONT KNOW WHEN TO LOOK. "LOOK TOWARD THE SEA, AND COME BACK AND TELL ME WHAT'S GOING ON OUT THERE." OBADIAH WENT OUT THERE AND LOOKED, AND SAID: "THERE'S NOTHING OUT THERE. I DONT SEE ANYTHING - NOT A THING." ELIJAH SAID: "GO BACK AGAIN - TAKE ANOTHER LOOK."

I REMEMBER WHEN I WAS A CHILD AND MY MOTHER WOULD SEND ME TO FIND SOMETHING - TO GET SOMETHING - AND, I'D GO IN THE ROOM AND LOOK, AND I CANT FIND IT. AND, I'D COME BACK AND SAY: MA MA! I CANT FIND WHAT YOU SENT ME FOR. (YOU OUGHT TO HAVE SAID THAT SOME TIME! YOU WENT TO LOOK FOR SOMETHING AND COULDN'T FIND IT!) AND, YOU KNOW WHAT MY MOTHER WOULD SAY? SHE WOULDN'T WHIP ME. SHE WOULDN'T ABUSE ME. SHE'D SAY: "SON, GO BACK. TAKE ANOTHER LOOK." AND, I WENT BACK AND I TOOK ANOTHER LOOK - AND, I FOUND WHAT I WAS LOOKING FOR. HALLELUJAH. HALLELUJAH. HALLELUJAH, THIS MORNING.

OBADIAH WENT BACK AND TOOK ANOTHER LOOK, THE SECOND TIME. AND, ELIJAH SAID: "WHAT DO YOU SEE OUT THERE?" HE SAID: "A LITTLE CLOUD. I SEE A LITTLE SPECK OUT THERE. I SEE IT NOW - AND, I'VE NEVER SEEN IT BEFORE. JUST A LITTLE BIT, OUT THERE." ELIJAH SAID: "WELL, THAT'S ENOUGH. IF MY GOD GIVES YOU A LITTLE BIT - THAT'S ENOUGH. YOU DONT HAVE TO GO BACK ANYMORE." HALLELUJAH. IT'S GOOD TO TAKE ANOTHER LOOK. "GO TELL AHAB, THAT GOD IS GOING TO SEND SOME RAIN DOWN HERE. TELL HIM TO GET HIS CHARIOT READY."

I'M REMINDED, NOW, ABOUT THE PROPHET WHEN HE WENT DOWN TO THE WIDOW'S HOME AND THE FAMINE WAS STILL ON - AND, HE WENT IN AND SAID: "WELL, I WANT YOU TO JUST MAKE A LITTLE CAKE. I'M HUNGRY." SHE SAID: "WELL, THE GRAIN IS ALMOST GONE - NOT MUCH MORE LEFT IN THERE - JUST A LITTLE BIT. AND, THE OIL HAS RUN LOW TOO." HE SAID: "WELL, HONEY - THE MAN OF GOD SAID, GIVE HIM THE FIRST CAKE. GOD WILL BLESS YOU, IF YOU GIVE HIM FIRST." "SEEK YE FIRST THE KINGDOM OF GOD AND HIS RIGHTEOUSNESS, AND ALL THESE THINGS WILL BE ADDED UNTO YOU." HALLELUJAH. SHE SAID: "WELL, MY SON AND I ARE GOING EAT THAT LITTLE CAKE, AND DIE. BUT, IF YOU TELL ME TO DO THIS - (HER LITTLE SON WAS SHEDDING TEARS AND SAYING: "I'M HUNGRY - I'M HUNGRY, MA MA."). SHE SAID: "WELL, SON, I'VE GOT TO GIVE IT TO HIM - HE'S A MAN OF GOD AND HE TOLD ME WHAT TO DO - AND, I'VE GOT TO DO IT - BECAUSE GOD, THROUGH HIM, HAS SPOKEN TO ME."

IT PAYS TO HEAR GOD'S TRUE SERVANT. AMEN. I'M NOT TALKING ABOUT A QUACK. I'M NOT TALKING ABOUT A FAKE. I'M NOT TALKING ABOUT SOMEBODY WHO'S A CONMAN. I'M TALKING ABOUT GOD'S SERVANT. GOD'S SERVANT - HEAR HIM WHEN HE TALKS TO YOU. SHE GOT THE LITTLE MEAL AND BEGAN TO STIR IT UP. THERE WASN'T ANY WATER DOWN THERE, YOU KNOW - THE ONLY WATER THAT SHE HAD WERE THE TEARS THAT SHE WAS DROPPING. EVERY TIME SHE WOULD STIR IT UP, A TEAR WOULD FALL. WEEPING - MAKING UP THE LAST CAKE. WHEN SHE GOT IT COOKED, SHE CARRIED IT TO HIM. HER LITTLE SON WAS FOLLOWING - TUGGING ON HER APRON AND SAYING: "MA MA - I'M HUNGRY." SHE SAID: "SONNY, I'VE GOT TO GIVE IT TO THE MAN OF GOD." SHE GAVE IT TO HIM AND HE SAT DOWN AND GOT READY TO EAT IT - AND, HE SAID: "HONEY - NOW, GO BACK AND TAKE ANOTHER LOOK. GO BACK, NOW - AND TAKE ANOTHER LOOK." HALLELUJAH. SHE SAID: "THERE'S NO NEED OF LOOKING IN THERE. BUT, IF YOU SAY TAKE ANOTHER LOOK - I'LL GO." AND, SHE WENT BACK OVER THERE - TOOK ANOTHER LOOK - AND THE MEAL WAS STILL THERE. HALLELUJAH. SHE LOOKED IN THE CRUSE AND THE CRUSE STILL HAD OIL IN IT - IT NEVER RAN OUT. GOD WILL PROVIDE FOR HIS CHILDREN - YES HE WILL! I'M A WITNESS - HE WILL PROVIDE. GOD WILL TAKE CARE OF YOU - TAKE ANOTHER LOOK THIS MORNING. THE HEBREW BOYS TOOK ANOTHER LOOK - AND, WHEN THEY TOOK ANOTHER LOOK, THEY SAW FOUR - WHERE THERE HAD BEEN THREE. EZEKIEL TOOK ANOTHER LOOK - AND, WHERE THE DRY BONES WERE, THE BONES GOT UP FROM THERE. HALLELUJAH. HE TOOK ANOTHER LOOK. YES - HALLELUJAH! THANK GOD

THIS MORNING. EZEKIEL TOOK ANOTHER LOOK. AND, WHEN HE TOOK IT, HE SAID HE SAW A WHEEL. YOU DONT KNOW WHAT I'M TALKING ABOUT. A WHEEL - IN THE MIDDLE OF A WHEEL. THE BIG WHEEL MOVES BY FAITH - THE LITTLE WHEEL MOVES BY THE GRACE OF GOD. WHEEL - IN A WHEEL. WHEN ISAIAH HAD FOUND OUT THAT AZIAH HAD DIED, HE SAID HE'D TAKE ANOTHER LOOK. THAT'S WHY I'M TALKING ABOUT TAKIN ANOTHER LOOK. I WANT TO CONVINCE YOU ALL TO DONT BE DISCOURAGED, OVER THE FIRST LOOK. THAT'S WHY I'M TALKING ABOUT IT THIS MORNING. IT WILL GIVE YOU SOMETHING TO STAND UPON, WHEN THINGS GO AGAINST YOU. HALLELUJAH. WHEN YOU'RE DOWN TRODDEN AND THINGS DONT GO RIGHT - TAKE ANOTHER LOOK. WHEN YOU'RE PERSECUTED - TAKE ANOTHER LOOK. WHEN THEY'RE LIEING ON YOU - TAKE ANOTHER LOOK. WHEN THEY DECEIVE YOU - TAKE ANOTHER LOOK. YE--S! TAKE ANOTHER LOOK. YOU KNOW, SOMEBODY TOOK A LOOK - AND, THEY KEPT ON LOOKING UNTIL THEY SAW A HUNDRED AND FORTY-FOUR THOUSAND. HALLELUJAH. BUT, GO BACK - TAKE ANOTHER LOOK. AND, THEY WENT BACK - TOOK ANOTHER LOOK - "AND I SAW A NUMBER, THAT NO MAN - NO MAN, CAN NUMBER." HALLELUJAH. HALLELUJAH. HALLELUJAH.

Amen.

APPENDIX TEN

EPISCOPAL ADDRESS
of
The Right Reverend Herbert Bell Shaw
149th Session
New York Annual Conference
African Methodist Episcopal Zion Church
Wednesday, June 17, 1970

"Grace be unto you, and peace, from God our Father, and from the Lord Jesus Christ. I thank my God always on your behalf, for the grace of God which is given you by Jesus Christ; That in everything ye are enriched by him, in all utterance, and in all knowledge; Even as the testimony of Christ was confirmed in you; So that ye come behind in no gift; waiting for the coming of our Lord Jesus Christ: Who shall also confirm you unto the end, that ye may be blameless in the day of our Lord Jesus Christ. God is faithful, by whom ye were called unto the fellowship of his Son Jesus Christ our Lord. Now I beseech you, brethren, by the name of our Lord Jesus Christ, that ye all speak the same thing, and that there be no divisions among you; but that ye be perfectly joined together in the same mind and in the same judgment."

I Corinthians 1:3-10

I am more than happy and honored to officially greet you today as I attempt to deliver to you this Episcopal Address which constitutes the 60th of my episcopacy. I give thanks to almighty God for the gifts and preservation of life, health and strength during the past 12 months. The days have been long and the nights sometimes weary, but through it all we have been marvelously sustained by His grace, mercy and guidance. We now recite with the hymnist, Charles Wesley:

> "What troubles have we seen,
> What conflicts have we passed,
> Fightings without and fears within,
> Since we assembled last:
>
> But out of all the Lord
> Hath brought us by His love;
> And still He doth His help afford,
> And hides our life above."

Our theme for this conference was chosen after much thought and prayer. It should have abundant meaning and significance for us as we strive to 'serve the present age, our calling to fulfill."

"The Spirit of the Lord is upon me.
1. He hath appointed me to preach the gospel to the poor.
2. He hath sent me to heal the broken-hearted.
3. To preach deliverance to the captives.
4. The recovering of sight to the blind.
5. To set at liverty them that are bruised.
6. To preach the acceptable year of the Lord."

Luke 4:18-19.

This is our task, this is our duty, this is our challenge. To do any less would surely constitute a reprehensible repudiation of our sacred calling. Here the duty and obligation of the Minister is clearly defined and eloquently presented. It is our inescapable duty to articulate and implement the same with emphasis and certainty every day and in every way. This six point program must form the foundation of our ministerial lives. "Et Moriturus est." (the die is cast.) There can be no turning back because, "The spirit of the Lord is upon us."

Remember the words of Harriet du Autermont:

"No vision and you perish.
No ideal, and you're lost;
Your heart must ever cherish
Some faith at any cost.

Some hope, some dream to cling to,
Some rainbow in the sky,
Some melody to sing to,
Some service that is high."

Our world is struggling in the midst of inevitable change. The twentieth century is truly pregnant with the babes of change. None of the changes are victims of premature birth. Many of us are knowledgeable of the fact that most of the changes are suffering because of delayed birth. We observe that there is a determined effort on the part of some to delay, prevent and sabotage the normal and absolutely essential change from repression to freedom, from discrimination to equality, from prejudice to justice, from war to peace, from hate to love, from spiritual ineptitude to spiritual plenitude. This attitude is both ruinous and corruptive and if not speedily corrected can only eventuate in the destruction of our total social fabric. In the progressive course of human events change must be anticipated, invited, encouraged, and when necessary demanded, if we are to enjoy any semblance of cohesion in our society without which our civilization cannot survive.

America is suffering in the throes of ferment and travail because too many who have been entrusted with national leadership are betraying the faith of the founding Fathers of this nation. This is true from the White House down to the lowest echelon of our public officials. This blatant and reckless disregard for the tenets of our Declaration of Independence, Bill of Rights and Constitution have caused the American flag to be dipped in the blood of youth on the campuses of our state colleges at Orangeburg, South Carolina, Kent, Ohio, and Jackson, Mississippi. The blood of these youth, along with many others, cry aloud from the ground for a new birth of freedom. Such iniquitous acts of bloody repression only rape our "Lady of Liberty" on lonely Bedloe Island as she stands there in shame with her slowly diminishing torch in her enfeebled hand.

The thunderous roar of guns and cannons along with the chilling sound of death from the skies continues in Vietnam. While holding the olive branch of peace in one hand, someone forgetting the campaign promise of ending the war, expands the conflict into Cambodia with an appalling toll of dead and dying. The lot of those honorable dead was not to reason why, theirs was but to do and die. The onerous sound of rapid machine gun fire, interspersed with the sound of cannon and missile is heard again in the Holy land and the ground once made sacred by the footprints of Jesus is again baptized with the blood of those He came to save. The Star of the East seems to be in eclipse and the hammer and sickle arising over the distant horizon.

In the midst of all the change and decay which is around, we see God still works His sovereign will and the Black man, with his religion, culture and civilization reaching back through the centuries emerges as the hope of the "New Day Aborning."

> "Ye fearful saints, fresh courage take
> The clouds ye so much dread
> Are big with mercy and shall break
> In blessings on your head.
>
> Blind unbelief is sure to err
> And scan His work in vain
> God is His own interpreter
> And He will make it plain."

There is a new man in our midst and he is black, "old things are passed away and all things are become new." "Forgetting the things that are past, we press forward to the mark of our high calling which is in Christ Jesus." We have taken off the old man and put on the new. We have been born again.

There are many organizations, some old, some new. We like and approve the method, technique and strategy of some while we fail to understand, appreciate and condone others. But all seem to be aggressive, creative, and full of purpose. They seem to be consumed with an undying passion to unshackle the black man so that he might go about his sacred duty of saving America and the world from ignominious suicide. Let us remember that, "the wind bloweth where its listeth and we hear the sound thereof but can'st not tell whence it cometh nor whither it goeth, so it is with every new creature who is born of God, "and the black man is a New Creature. God's word is true.

> "His purposes will ripen fast,
> Unfolding every hour;
> The bud may have a bitter taste,
> But sweet will be the flower."

I now call your attention to a new emphasis which is suggested for the 4th Sunday in June, traditionally known as, "Children's Day." Since this Sunday comes just before the 4th of July that is designated as "Independence Day," commemorating the adoption, signing and issue of the unanimous Declaration of the Thirteen United States of America by Congress, July 4, 1776 which reads in part, "When in the course of human events it becomes necessary for one people to dissolve the political bands which have connected them with another, and to assume among the powers of the earth, the separate and equal station to which the laws of Nature and of Nature's God entitle them, a decent respect to the opinions of mankind, requires that they should declare the causes which impel them to the separation. We hold these truths to be self-evident, that all men are created equal, that they are endowed by their Creator with certain unalienable Rights, that among these are Life, Liberty and the pursuit of Happiness. That to secure these rights, Governments are instituted among Men, deriving their just powers from the consent of the governed. That whenever any Form of Government becomes destructive of these ends, it is the Right of the People to alter or to abolish it, and to institute new government, laying its foundation on such principles and organizing its powers in such form, as to them shall seem most likely to effect their Safety and Happiness. Indeed this most sacred and prestigious document which forms the very foundation of our national existence should be removed from the shelves of indifference and neglect with the utmost prestisimo. It is for this reason that on the 4th Sunday in June we will present to the world our "Black Declaration of Independence." This declaration will call for a new emphasis, a new dedication, a new knowledge, a new concern for all Americans who are being increasingly denied their God-given rights by degenerate demagogues who consistently and persistently demean the high office of President, Vice President, Senator, Congressman, Governor and State Legislator. We stand and salute the America whose good is crowned with true brotherhood, and will toil and pray until this becomes a living truth from sea to shining sea. It is our hope that the "Black Declaration of Independence" will be read from every pulpit, read at the site of the Liberty Bell in Philadelphia, read at the feet of the Statue of Liberty, read on the floors of Congress, read at the White House, read in the Congressional Library, read in every state legislature throughout the nation, and above all, not only read, but engraved in the hearts of our countrymen. Let us contemplate the following lines from James Clarence Mangan ----

GONE IN THE WIND

"Solomon! where is thy throne? It is gone in the wind.
Babylon! where is thy might? It is gone in the wind.
Like the swift shadows of Noon, like the dreams of the blind,
Vanish the glories and pomps of the earth in the wind.

Man! canst thou build upon aught in the pride of thy mind?
Wisdom will teach thee that nothing can tarry behind;
Though there be thousand bright actions embalmed and enshrined,
Myriads and millions of brighter are snow in the wind.

Solomon! where is thy throne? It is gone in the wind.
Babylon! where is thy might? It is gone in the wind.
All that the genius of Man hath achieved and designed
Waits for its hour to be dealt with as dust by the wind."

The A.M.E. Zion Church again stands at the cross-roads. There are many painful decisions to be made concerning our aims, our structure, our polity, our ritual and our General Rules.

Commissions have been appointed by the Board of Bishops to study and evaluate the whole field of programmatics involved in our church and to suggest procedures that will make our church relevant to all the areas of need existing within our great constituency. Those of us who are interested must find the finances necessary for such a self-study of the church and evaluation.

The matter of COCU is before us and we must meet its challenge intelligently and fearlessly. We must carefully study all of its implications and ramifications. We must decide whether we are ready for the bells to toll for the demise of Varick's Church which is the church of our love and choice. COCU began with the meaning of Consultation on Church Union. Now it has metamorphosed into the meaning of Church of Christ Uniting. I hesitate to predict the next metamorphosis.

Death has entered our ranks since the last Annual Conference. The following faithful, loyal and dedicated ministers of the New York Conference now rest from their labors; Reverends S. N. Dunbar, E. S. Travalee, Franklin Lewis, and Annie J. Smith. God grant rest to their souls and peace to their ashes.

The Saints Who Died of Christ Possest

"The Saints who die of Christ possest,
Enter into immediate rest:
For them no farther test remains
Of purging fires and torturing pains:

Who trusting in their Lord depart,
Cleans'd from all sin, and pure in heart
The bliss unmixt, the glorious prize,
They find with Christ in paradise.

Close follow'd by their works they go,
Their Master's purchas'd joy to know;
Their works enhance the bliss prepar'd
And each hath its distinct reward:

Yet glorified by grace alone
They cast their crowns before the throne
And fill the echoing courts above
With praises of redeeming Love."

Charles Wesley

stand in the very vanguard of our Methodism. I state without fear of successful contradiction that the New York Conferences have achieved distinct leadership in the A.M.E. Zion Church. We have cheerfully embraced our opportunities and unflinchingly met the challenges of the urban communities. We have been weighed in the balances and have not been found wanting, therefore our Kingdom shall not be divided between the Medes and the Persians for we ourselves are not divided. Our youth have caught the vision of the Holy Grail and are moving acceptably and unerringly toward the goals of self-improvement, self-determination, identity and relativity. They have not only endulged the art of destructive criticism, but are projecting new methods, new ideas, and new approaches for the progressive and creative way in which we might solve old problems and enter the third world with dramatic new dimensions and ideals. This is all done under the able and dedicated leadership of our Christian Education Directors of whom Mrs. Annette Whitted is the Conference President. A word of sincere thanks to these molders of the budding men and women of the New generation.

Our Youth Honor Banquet in the New York Conference will be held at Patricia Murphy's elegant celebration center. The youth chose the place and named the price. This is their "thing". Let us support it 100%.

The Western New York Conference held their Youth Honor Banquet in April at the Casino in Saratoga Springs.

The General Convention on Christian Education will be held at Livingstone College, beginning the First Sunday in August. Let us send the largest delegation ever to this great convention, the theme of which is, "The Black Man's Contribution to World Culture."

TELLING A NEGLECTED STORY

Our M. Ardelle Shaw Camp appears to be at the threshold of a new era. The magnificent response of our Ministers and Laymen is indeed both refreshing and encouraging. There seems to be a genuine ground-swell of interest and concern for our Camp. I am pleased to express my gratitude to the Pastors and Laymen who are providing camperships for our youth who desire to get away from the hot and unattractive streets of the City. This really constitutes a magnanimous spirit on your part, of which you should feel justly proud. It appears that our Camp will be filled to capacity each week of the season.

We are very grateful to the Youth of the Western New York Conference who under the leadership of their Pastors and Directors of Christian Education, with Mrs. Edna Miller, the capable Conference President, contributed the amount of $4,000.00 toward the purchasing of the Camp. This certainly constitutes a giant step in cooperation between the youth of both conferences.

We express profound appreciation to Mrs. DeVera Johnson Lockhart for the gift of a very useful station wagon to the Camp, and to Mrs. Naomi Epps and Mrs. Louise Wilkerson for securing a gift of beautiful furniture from the S & H Green Stamps enterprise for the camp.

We now pause to express our appreciation and thanks to the three great Managers and motivating forces of our Camp, the Reverends Andrew H. Whitted, Belvie H. Jackson, Jr., and Eldridge Gittens. These are three of the busiest pastors in our conference. Yet they find the time to devote to the development of this unique facility for our youth and adults. They give this service without cost, for we cannot yet find the money to pay for their services. As they so unselfishly serve, they may know that their star rises ever higher and higher in the galaxy of the great heroes in Zion.

...ies. Each person attending the Camp Meeting will be expected to contribute $...00, and will be guest at a free fellowship old fashioned dinner with plenty of ...e punch to keep you cool. We are requesting the pastors to actively assist i... ...moting this unique service.

... are recommending that we designate a Youth Sunday, and a Woman's Day ...day at the Camp. The emphasis here will be cultural and ecological. Willis ...llen Bryan said that, "he who in love of nature holds communion with her ...ible forms, she speaks a various language," and Shakespeare opines that the... ...e books in running brooks, sermons in stones, and good in everything. The ...itribution of $5.00 is expected from each and full participation in fellowship, ...od and comfort assured. It is our hope and expectation that more than a ...usand persons will visit the Camp on each of these special days.

...solicit and urge the volunteering of Camp Patrons and Camp Boosters who ...l manifest special interest in the development of the Camp.

...r Sesqui-Centennial Celebration of the New York Conference is now assuming ...full dimension of programatical accomplishment. Words are futile when I ...empt to express my gratitude and appreciation to the Reverend Dr. V. Loma ...Clair for his dedication and leadership exemplified as Co-Ordinator of our ...squi-Centennial Celebration. I also express similar gratitude and apprecia-...i to the Chairmen of all Committees for expertise shown in their accomplish-...nts. This Celebration will reflect unusual credit upon all of us as we work

TELLING A NEGLECTED STORY

I am recommending that we choose and set aside a Sunday to be known as "Revival Camp Meeting Sunday" at the Camp. On this Sunday we shall have a great outdoor revival service in the old fashion way. I am requesting the Missionary Evangelists of the Conference to take charge of these services and plan the services of the day. There will be great sermons from the Evangelists, and great revival song services. Each person attending the Camp Meeting will be expected to contribute $5.00, and will be guest at a free fellowship old fashioned dinner with plenty of free punch to keep you cool. We are requesting the pastors to actively assist in promoting this unique service.

We are recommending that we designate a Youth Sunday, and a Woman's Day Sunday at the Camp. The emphasis here will be cultural and ecological. William Cullen Bryan said that, "he who in love of nature holds communion with her visible forms, she speaks a various language," and Shakespeare opines that there are books in running brooks, sermons in stones, and good in everything. The contribution of $5.00 is expected from each and full participation in fellowship, good and comfort assured. It is our hope and expectation that more than a thousand persons will visit the Camp on each of these special days.

We solicit and urge the volunteering of Camp Patrons and Camp Boosters who will manifest special interest in the development of the Camp.

Our Sesqui-Centennial Celebration of the New York Conference is now assuming the full dimension of programatical accomplishment. Words are futile when I attempt to express my gratitude and appreciation to the Reverend Dr. V. Lorna St. Clair for his dedication and leadership exemplified as Co-Ordinator of our Sesqui-Centennial Celebration. I also express similar gratitude and appreciation to the Chairmen of all Committees for expertise shown in their accomplishments. This Celebration will reflect unusual credit upon all of us as we work

175

together to make it the most auspicious event in our history.

I now quote from an editorial published in our STAR OF ZION, which was written by our editor, Dr. M. B. Robinson.

NEW YORK CONF. SESQUI-CENTENNIAL

"That the New York Conference -- set apart June 21, 1821 -- is celebrating its one hundred and fifty years of service and existence is quite proper.

"This our Mother Conference has in many respects, led the Connection for a number of years. She still holds her head proudly and carries a large share of Connectional responsibility.

"The conference has had through the years Episcopal giants to guide her destiny, thus she has continued to move forward. Some of the Superintendents or Bishops serving were James Varick, Christopher Rush, William H. Bishop, George A. Spywood, J. W. Hood, Alexander Walters, Josiah Samuel Caldwell, Lynwood Westinghouse Kyles, William Jacobs Walls and Herbert Bell Shaw.

"The conference has, perhaps experienced its greatest growth from Bishop Caldwell's tenure to the present time. The conference has grown to the extent that another Presiding Elder's District has been added making three in all. The General Conference delegation has also grown from ten in 1932 to fourteen in 1968. Some of the leading personalities of the race and Church have been and are now members of the great New York Conference.

"The present Presiding Bishop Herbert Bell Shaw had established a reputation for progress and Connectional productivity when the Board of Bishops elected him to complete the unexpired term of Dr. T. W. Wallace, Secretary of Home Missions, Brotherhood Pensions and Relief. Dr. Shaw was later elected a Bishop and eventually appointed to the Mother Conference where he is demonstrating in a grand way his leadership abilities. The observing of the Sesqui-Centennial is a giant step forward.

"Zion -- all Zion, rejoices with leaders and members of the Mother Conference because of their glowing success and promising future. We join with Bishop Shaw in 'Invoking the blessings of Almighty God, and commend this celebration and undertaking to the active and liberal support and enthusiasm of our constituents and friends everywhere.'"

Our Laymen are certainly among the greatest in our entire Connection. Many of them hold unique positions of leadership in many of our National Church organizations and connectional institutions. They are loyal. They are concerned. They are generous. They are cooperative and they are lovely.

Mr. J. Carl Canty is the Conference President of our Laymen's Council and we are proud of his leadership. The District Presidents stand in the forefront of dedicated leadership. I am happy to salute them and all our laymen in all our churches for their unstinted support of the building of the Kingdom of God in Zion.

The W. H. &F. M. Society ranks a place at the head of the Class in all Zion Methodism. Their work and concern for missions is above and beyond the call of ordinary duty. They truly lead as others follow.

Mrs. Minnie D. Hurley, our General Treasurer, is one of the best General Officers in our church. She excells in leadership, not only on the General Church level, but also on the District and in the local church. All our District Officers and local Missionaries are superb.

I wish to express my gratitude and profound appreciation to the Presiding Elders, Pastors and Laymen who proved their missionary concern by making sacrificial contributions for our work in Jamaica. Your contributions have made the difference between success and failure, the difference between joy and sorrow, the difference between tears and smiles, the difference between the night of disappointment and the morning of accomplishment. "Let us not be weary in welldoing, for in due season we shall reap, if we faint not." I again appeal to you for...

In the area of achievements and projects we note tremendous and spectacular progress.

The Reverend Luico C. Caldwell has led his congregation in liquidation of the mortgage incurred for the modernization and beautification of St. Francis Church ahead of schedule thus saving the church several thousand dollars in interest. Orchids of praise to this Pastor and congregation.

The Reverend Madison J. McRae has excelled himself in leading his congregation in expanding the Foster Memorial Church. It is now a church of great beauty. Rev. McRae did most of the work himself with the help of his people. This was a pay as you go project. Orchids of praise to this Pastor and congregation.

The Reverend T. H. Brooks is leading his congregation in the erection of a new church at Hudson, N. Y. This replaces a building that was over 100 years old. This congregation has taken on a new spirit as it takes its place among the progressive forces of the New York Conference. Orchids of praise to this Pastor and congregation.

The Reverend Ulysses S. Jackson has led his congregation in the completion of the Church on the Hill at tremendous cost. This church is not only the Church on the Hill but it now takes its place as the Church on Top of the Hill. This church is now associated in a 3½ million dollar housing project. Orchids of praise to this Pastor and congregation.

The Reverend Eldridge Gittins has led his congregation in the purchasing of a beautiful parsonage which I had the privilege of dedicating on Sunday, June 7. On the same day the Bishop, pastor and congregation broke ground for the erection of a $181,000.00 Day Care Center and a $287,000.00 addition to the Church which will make it one of the most beautiful and accommodative in the area. Orchids of praise to this Pastor and congregation.

TELLING A NEGLECTED STORY

The Reverend Lillian T. Brunner has led her congregation in making the Mother Walls Church a beautiful edifice of worship. They have installed lovely pews, pulpit furniture and articles to increase the atmosphere of worship which the Bishop dedicated on June 7th. Orchids of praise to this Pastor and congregation.

It was our privilege to dedicate the new pews and pulpit furniture at Walters Memorial Church. This achievement was wrought under the leadership of the Reverend Paul F. Thurston. This pastor also distinguishes himself in community leadership. Orchids of praise to this Pastor and congregation.

The Reverend Frank E. Jones displays unique leadership at the Washington Street Church, Newburgh. Here we have a multi-million dollar housing project under construction under the sponsorship of our Church. This project is named in honor of our first Bishop James Varick. Orchids of praise to this Pastor and congregation.

The Reverend Andrew E. Whitted distinguishes himself as a leader in Zion with his congregation in the construction of the Carrington Arms Apartments along with one of our most modern church edifices at a cost of approximately three million dollars. Orchids of praise to this Pastor and congregation.

The Reverend Dr. Reuben L. Speaks continues to display rare leadership at the First A.M.E. Zion Church. The cost of renovation and modernization now amounts to $345,000.00. The latest project is the renewal of the exterior of the church at a cost of 30 thousand dollars. This is a cash project for this loyal congregation. Orchids of praise to Pastor and congregation.

Our Mother Church, Mother A.M.E. Zion, continues its magnificent march of progress under the dynamic and astute leadership of the Reverend Dr. George W. McMurray. This great church continues to make noteworthy cash contributions to many churches in this conference. The Mother Church now assumes undisputed leadership in Harlem with the government approved construction of a multi-million dollar multi-purpose Community Center. The Mother Church is now in the process of acquiring one of the most beautiful parsonage in the denomination. Orchilds of praise to Pastor and congregation for this unique progress.

Distinguished leadership is evidence by the following Pastors for the perfecting of plans for the construction of new church edifices and or housing projects: The Reverends Ralph W. Guillette, Mt. Hope, White Plains, Belvie Jackson, Greater Centennial, Mt. Vernon, Petty D. McKinney, Smith Street, Poughkeepsie, Eugene McKenzie, Naomi Church, Coney Island, W. J. Jiles, Barry Avenue Church, Mamaroneck, Dr. Frank E. Churchill, Greater Hood Memorial Church, Manhattan, and the Reverend R. W. Fernanders who is giving us another first rank beautiful edifice, the Metropolitan Church at Yonkers, W. D. Hogans of Calvary A. M. E. Zion in Jamaica and his congregation are now raising funds for the erection of a new educational building. Orchids of praise to these noble pastors and their progressive congregations.

In the Western New York Conference the wheels of progress are turning rapidly. Under the wise leadership of P. E. E. M. Williams, the congregation at Troy has purchased a beautiful new church and parsonage at a cost of 48 thousand dollars which was paid in cash. This property is valued at 150 thousand dollars. This acquisition places Zion up front in Troy. Orchids to the Pastor and congregation.

In Buffalo, N.Y., we received a great church, 15 room parsonage, and two car garage as a gift from the United Methodist Church. These buildings stand upon a perfect triangle of land in the center of the cultural area of the city and the property is valued at one million dollars. Under the leadership of the Reverend

Milton A. Williams and the pastors of the City of Buffalo this church is making phenominal progress with the support of all the pastors and congregations in the conference. We are now in process of receiving another church located in Rochester as a gift from the United Methodist Church. This property is valued at one half million dollars. Orchids of praise and gratitude to Bishop Ward of the United Methodist Church and the Western New York Conference.

The wives of our Ministers are lovely, sympathetic and full of understanding. Our pastors are the greatest because their wives are the greatest. Many of them work at the side of their husbands, thus achieving unusual success as a result of their teamwork. I thank them for their cooperation and for kindnesses, courtesies and hospitality shown me as I sojourned in their lovely homes. Truly they have made me feel at home when I was far away from home.

Now for a brief word of appreciation to our Missionary Supervisor, Mrs. M. Ardelle Shaw, and my beloved wife, Ardelle. Thank you for your prayers, your understanding, your wisdom and your love. From my heart I send you an orchid of thanks.

Miss Frances Elizabeth Atkins is indeed one of the finest secretaries that any Bishop or Conference could wish. She is indeed of great value. Her labor is unending, her smile is unfading and her patience is of long endurance. I thank you for your support in helping to compensate for her services. But, I say to you and to her that money can never pay the debt of love and appreciation we owe. I close by repeating that, "The Spirit of the Lord is upon us" and "Who shall separate us from the love of Christ? shall tribulation, or distress, or persecution, or famine, or nakedness, or peril, or sword? As it is written, For thy sake we are killed all the day long; we are accounted as sheep for the slaughter. Nay, in all these things we are more than conquerors through him that loved us. For I am persuaded that neither death, nor life, nor angels, nor principalities, nor powers, nor things present, nor things to come, nor height, nor depth, nor any other creature, shall be able to separate us from the love of God, which is in Christ Jesus our Lord."

Romans 8:35-39

BE STRONG

"   Be strong!
We are not here to play, to dream, to drift,
We have hard work to do, and loads to lift.
Shun not the struggle, face it, 'tis God's gift.

      Be strong!
Say not the days are evil - who's to blame!
And fold the hands and acquiese - O shame!
Stand up, speak out, and bravely, in God's name.

      Be strong!
It matters not how deep entrenched the wrong,
How hard the battle goes, the day, how long;
Faint not, fight on! To-morrow comes the song."

Maltbie D. Babcock

BIBLIOGRAPHY

Agosto, Efrain. Servant Leadership: Jesus & Paul. St. Louis, Missouri: Chalice Press, 2005

Ahlstrom, Sydney E. A Religious History of the American People. New Haven: Yale University Press, 1972.

Andrews, Dee E. The Methodists and Revolutionary America, 1760-1800: The Shaping of an Evangelical Culture. New Jersey: Princeton University Press, 2000

Armstrong, James David. A Brief Historical Survey of the African Methodist Episcopal Zion Church, (North Carolina: The A.M.E. Zion Historical Society, 2004.

James David Armstrong. A Review of a History of John Wesley A.M.E. Zion Church, Washington D.C

Author Unknown. Bishop William J. Walls "Up From Nature's Pulpit in Zion's Echoes Vol..II No.1 Sept.1949

Bacon, Leonard Woolsey. A History of American Christianity. New York: The Christian Literature Company, 1897

Blackaby, Henry & Richard. Spiritual Leadership: Moving People on to God's Agenda. Nashville, Tennessee: Broadman & Holman Publishers,2001

Bonner, Revs. H.D. & L.L. Smith et al. Reverence of a Senior Bishop First Episcopal District: First Church 1965

Borden, Henry Warner and P.C. Kenney, Editors. American Church History. Nashville: Abingdon Press, 1998

Bracey, John H., Jr. and Harley, Sharon (Editors) Papers of the NAACP Supplement to Part 1, 1966-1970 A Microfilm Project of University Publications of America. An imprint of LexisNexis Academic & Library Solutions, Bethesda, MD

Bradley, David Henry Sr. A History of the A.M.E. ZION CHURH: Part II 1872-1968: (Nashville: Tennessee, The Parthenon Press, 1970

Bradley, David H. Report of the A.M.E. Zion Historical Society June 1958- May 31-1959. Board of Bishops & The Connectional Council of The A.M.E. Zion Church, Springfield, Mass. July 30, 1959

Brauer, Jerald C. Protestantism in America: A Narrative History. Philadelphia: The Westminster Press, 1953.

Bullock, Bessie. Reverend Louis E. Sanders St. Charles AM.E. Zion Church, 432 Valentine Avenue, Sparkill, NY 10976, (no date)

Burke, Emory Steven General Editor et al. The History of American Methodism, Vol. III New York: Abingdon Press, 1964.

Cannon, Katie G. Katie's Canon: Womanism and the Soul of the Black Community. New York: Continuum Publishing, 1995

Carroll, H.K., Watkins, LL.D. and W.T. The Methodist Book Concern, 1923 www. kansasheritage.org/um/asbury.

Daugherty, Ruth A. General Commission on Christian Unity and Interreligious Concerns, UMC in Pan Methodist Commission: One Voice For Christ: The Wesleyan Family. Charlotte, North Carolina, 2007.

Frank, Thomas Edward. The Discourse Of Leadership and the Practice of Administration Atlanta, Georgia: Emory University, 2002

Fulop, Timothy E. and Albert J. Raboteau (Editors). African-American Religion: Interpretive Essays in History & Culture. New York; Routledge, 1977.

Gaustad, Edwin and Leigh Schmidt. The Religious History of America: The Heart of The American Story from Colonial Times to Today. San Francisco, CA: Harper Collins, 2002.

Green, V.H.H. John Wesley. New York: University Press of America, 1987.

Hall, Stephen G., Faithful Account of the Race: African American Historical Writing in Nineteenth-Century America, (Chapel Hill: The University of North Carolina Press 2009),

Hardt, Rev. Dr. Philip F. The Soul of Methodism: The Class Meeting in Early New York City Methodism. New York: University Press of America, Inc., 2000.

Hatch, Nathan O. and Wigger, John W. (Editors) Methodism and the Shaping of America Nashville, Tennessee: Kingswood Books, 2001.

Heitzenrater, Richard P. Wesley and the People Called Methodists. Nashville: Abingdon Press, 1995.
Hempton, David. Methodism: Empire of the Spirit. New Haven, Connecticut: Yale University Press, 2005.

History of American Methodism.

Hoggard, Bishop James Clinton. The African Methodist Episcopal Zion Church, 1972-1996: A Bicentennial Commemorative History. Charlotte, North Carolina: A.M.E. Zion Publishing House, 1998.

Holt, Ivan Lee. The Methodists of the World. New York: Editorial Department, Board of Missions and Church Extension of the Methodist Church, 1950.

TELLING A NEGLECTED STORY

Hood, James Walker Hood. 1831-1918 Sketch of the Early History of the African Methodist Episcopal Zion Church with Jubilee Souvenir And Appendix: Electronic Edition © This work is the property of the University of North Carolina at Chapel Hill. It may be used freely by individuals

Hood, Bishop J.W. One Hundred Years of the African Methodist Episcopal Zion Church: The Centennial of African Methodism. New York: A.M.E. Zion Book Concern, 1895.

Hudson, Winthrop S. Religion in America: An Historical Account of the Development Of American Religious Life. New York: MacMillan Publishing Company, 1992.

Idle, Christopher. The Journal of John Wesley. Michigan: Lion Publication Corp., 1986.

Jackson, E. Franklin. My Church: Hand Book for A.M.E. Zion Churchmen. Washington, D.C.: James A. Brown/John Wesley Church, 1953.

Jones, George H. (Editor) The Methodist Primer. Nashville, Tennessee: Methodist Evangelistic Material, ND.

Jones, Lawrence Neale. African Americans and the Christian Churches 1619-1860. Cleveland: The Pilgrim Press, 2007.

Lincoln, C. Eric and Lawrence H. Mamiya. The Black Church in the African American Experience. Durham, North Carolina: Duke University Press, 1999.

Lyerly, Cynthia Lynn. Methodism and the Southern Mind 1770-1810 New York: Oxford University Press, 1998.

McAlpine, Campbell. The Leadership of Jesus Kent, England: Sovereign World Ltd. 1982.

McCoy, Bishop James E. Episcopal Address – 2009, Alabama-Florida Episcopal District African Methodist Episcopal Zion Church, 2009

McEllhenney, John G. et al (Editors). United Methodists in America: A Compact History. Nashville: Abingdon Press, 1982.

Maize, George Wallace. "A Vision of Camp Dorothy walls: For the Negro Boy and Girl" in Reverence of a Senior Bishop by Revs. H.D. Bonner, L.L. Smith et al. First Episcopal District: First Church 1965

Marsh, Clive, Beck, Brian, Shier-Jones, Angela and Wareing, Helen. Methodist Theology Today: A Way Forward. New York: Continuum, 2004.

Maxwell, John C. The 21 indispensable Qualities of a Leader: Becoming the Person Others Will Want to Follow. Nashville: Thomas Nelson Publishers, 1999.

185

Tim Elmore. The Maxwell Leadership Bible (NKJV) Revised and Updated. Nashville: Thomas Nelson, 2007.

Miller, Basil. John Wesley. Minneapolis, Minnesota: Bethany House Publishers, 1943.

Moore, Bishop John Jamison. History of the A.M.E. Zion Church in America Charlotte, North
        Carolina: The A.M.E. Zion Historical Society, 2004

Nell. Mark A. A History of Christianity in the United States and Canada. Michigan:
        William B. Eerdman's Publishing Company, 1992.

Norwood, Frederick A. The Story of American Methodism: A History of the United Methodists   and Their Relations. New York: Abingdon Press, 1974

Odukoya, Rev. Dr. Adebola T. Spottswood AME Zion Church: 58 Years if Faithful testimony. Denver, Co., Spottswood AME Zion Church, 2005.

Olmstead, Clifton. History of Religions in the United States. Englewood Cliffs, NJ:
        Prentice Hall, Inc., 1960.

One Voice for Christ: The Wesleyan Family. Charlotte, North Carolina, 2007

Pan Methodist Commission, One Voice for Christ: The Wesleyan Family, (Charlotte, North Carolina, 2007

Parris, Peter J. Black Religious Leaders: Conflict In Unity. Louisville, KY: Westminster/John Knox Press, 1993

Payne, Wardell J. Directory of African Religious Bodies: A Compendium of the Howard
        University School of Divinity. Washington, D.C.: Howard University Press, 1995.

Pierce, Rev. Dr. Althea. Methodists: Living our Beliefs. A Presentation to the 114th
        Central Alabama Conference School of Prophets. October 15, 2009.

Queen II, Edward L. et al Editors. Encyclopedia of American Religious History. Third
        Edition. New York: Facts on File, Library of American History, Inc. 2009

Raboteau, Albert J. Slave Religion: The Invisible Institution in the Antebellum South. New York: Oxford University Press, 2004.

Reis, Oscar, Blacks in Colonial America, Jefferson, North Carolina: McFarland &N Company,
        Inc., Publishers, 1925.

Rush, Christopher. A Short Account of the Rise and Progress of the African Methodist Episcopal   Church in America. 21 Grand Street, New York: W. Marks, 1843.

Rush, Christopher and George Collins. A Short Account of the Rise and Progress of the African
        Methodist Episcopal Church in America Republished by the A.M.E. Zion Historical Society, Charlotte, NC 2000

TELLING A NEGLECTED STORY

Segovia, Fernando F. and Tolbert, Mary Ann (Editors) Reading from this Place Volume 1: Social Location and Biblical Interpretation in the United States. Minneapolis: Fortress Press, 1995

Sernett, Milton C. (Editor). African American Religious history: A Documentary Witness. Durham, NC: Duke University Press, 1999.

Smith, Theophus J. Conjuring Culture: Biblical Formations of Black America. New York: Oxford University Press, 1984.

Speaks, Ruben L. The Minister and His Task. Charlotte, North Carolina: A.M.E. Zion Publishing House, 1970.

Sweet, William Warren. Religion of the American Frontier 1783-1840: Vol. IV. New York: Cooper Square Publishers, Inc., 1964.

Taylor, Mattie W. Writer & Editor "Camp Dorothy Walls" in THE GOOD NEWS (Brooklyn, New York: First A.M.E Zion Church: January 2010)

_____ "Camp Dorothy Walls" in THE GOOD NEWS Brooklyn, New York: First A.M.E Zion Church: January 2010

The Book of Discipline of the African Methodist Episcopal Zion Church 2004. Charlotte, North Carolina: A.M.E. Zion Publishing House, 2005.

Thumma, Scott. Exploring the Mega Church Phenomena. San Francisco, CA: Wiley, 2007

Townsend, W.J. A New History of Methodism London: Hodder and Stoughton, 1909.

Vickers, John A. (Editor). A Dictionary of Methodism in Britain and Ireland. Great Britain: Biddles Ltd., Guildford and King's Lynn, 2000.

Walker, Bishop George W.C. "Revisiting the Traditions of our Fathers: Old Solutions to New Structures." The AME Zion Quarterly Review. James David Armstrong(Editor/Manager) Charlotte, North Carolina: 2005.

Walls, William J. Annual Address to the Annual Convention of National Fraternal Council of Churches. "Our Day Smiting A Passage through a World Like this"(Atlanta Georgia: Wheat Street Baptist   Church: April 3-4, 1953

_____ Report of the First Episcopal District, African Methodist Episcopal Zion Church at the Thirty-Sixth Quadrennial Session of the African Methodist Episcopal Zion Church   (Buffalo, New York: May-4-18, 1960), p.6

Bishop William J. Walls. Bishop William Walls, 'The Place of the Negro Church in History' in Bishop William Walls, Connectionalism and the Negro Church. (private papers held by the author,1954)

_____ Report of the First Episcopal District at the 38th Quadrennial Session, African Methodist Episcopal Zion Church,(Detroit, Michigan, 1968

_____. The A.M.E. Zion Church: It's Methodist Identity - Keynote Address at the
Quadrennial General Christian Education Convention (Salisbury, North Carolina: Livingstone College)July 31, 1966

_____   The African Methodist Episcopal Zion Church: Reality of the Black Church Charlotte, North Carolina: A.M.E. Zion Publishing House, 1974.

Wesley, John. Thoughts upon Slavery London, England: reprinted in Philadelphia, with notes
and sold by Joseph Crukshank, MD,CC

Wigger, John H Taking Heaven by Storm: Methodism and the Rise of Popular Christianity in America. Urbana, Illinois: University of Illinois Press, 1998.

INTERNET
Carroll, H.K. Carroll. And Watkins, W.T. The Methodist Book Concern. 1923
www.campdorothywalls.org
www.kansasheritage.org/um/asbury
www.chimneyrockpark.com
chadwohl@satucket.com; http://satucket.com
www.harriet tubman.com
www.christianleadrs.org
http://en.wikipedia.org/wiki/East_Ramapo_School_District
http://thebolesfamily.hubpags.com/hb/Slavery-and-the-Split-of-Methodism
www.kansasheritage.org/um/asbury.

PUBLICATIONS
The Washington Post, October 1, 1925The Star of Zion, Charlotte, North Carolina

TELLING A NEGLECTED STORY

North Carolina newspaper (name unidentified) Volume XLI--Number 498 dated Saturday, March 5, 1960: LIVINGSTONE IS INSPIRING IN LEADERSHIP: Bishop And Mrs. Walls Donate Site For Building

ADDRESSES

Walls, Rev. William J. Fraternal Address to the Bishops Fathers and Brethren of the General Conference of the Methodist Episcopal Church, South. May 1918.

Ibid.   A.M.E. Zion Sesquicentennial Lecte....... (N.Y. Conf.: 1821-1971

Bishop W.J. Walls The A.M.E. Zion Church: It's Methodist Identity - Keynote Address at the Quadrennial   General Christian Education Convention (Salisbury, North Carolina: Livingstone College)   July 31,   1966

INTERVIEW
Harrison D. Bonner. Interview. January 10, 2007, Waterbury, CT
Salome Walters. Interviews. April 2010, October 2011
Reverend Walter Brightman, Interview. September 2009

CORRESPONDENCE

Dr. Frank Brown, Dean, Hood Theological Seminary, Salisbury, NC to Bishop Herbert Bell Shaw, , September 1, 1964
Dr. George W. McMurray, Pastor, Mother AME Zion Church, New York, New York, to Bishop   Herbert Bell Shaw , Wilmington, NC dated June 1, 1971

www.ingramcontent.com/pod-product-compliance
Lightning Source LLC
Chambersburg PA
CBHW060526100426
42743CB00009B/1445